T0194158

God Uses the Foolish Things

Ron Momon

WESTBOW
PRESS®
A DIVISION OF THOMAS NELSON
& ZONDERVAN

WestBow Press books may be ordered through booksellers or by contacting:

WestBow Press
A Division of Thomas Nelson & Zondervan
1663 Liberty Drive
Bloomington, IN 47403
www.westbowpress.com
1 (866) 928-1240

ISBN: 978-1-5127-8694-1 (sc)
ISBN: 978-1-5127-8695-8 (hc)
ISBN: 978-1-5127-8693-4 (e)

Library of Congress Control Number: 2017907627

Print information available on the last page.

WestBow Press rev. date: 06/07/2017

Cover photo by Jeffrey Inman

Acknowledgments

Thanks to the late Apostle Johnny B. Watson Jr., of Sure Word Prophetic Ministries, for obeying God and giving me the confirming word on the writing of this book.

Contents

Foreword

On January 1, 2013, the Lord called out to me and said, "It's time." The Lord was advising me that it was time for me to step out and start the ministry that He had placed in my heart. At that very moment, I was overcome with joy and happiness, knowing that God would lead me and guide me to ensure success. However, a few weeks later, I found myself questioning God in reference to my calling. I felt unworthy due to my past, knowing that I had not always lived according to the word of God. I also found myself feeling intimidated and maybe even a little afraid; nevertheless, I knew very well that God had chosen me to lead this ministry. The Holy Spirit visited me supernaturally on more than one occasion, proving to me that He was with me.

However, Satan was trying to use my past as a means to keep me from obeying the will of God. One day toward the end of January, while speaking with a close friend, Ron Momon, he offered me the opportunity to read the introduction to this book. I begin to read, and wow! It was like a spiritual voice speaking to me, ministering to me. The words I read that day spoke directly to my heart. Every negative tactic that Satan had tried to inhibit the calling that God had placed on my life was challenged by the words I read. It spoke of forgiveness, callings, being chosen, and spiritual rejuvenation. It made mention of great men of the Bible who came from backgrounds that were less than perfect, yet they went on to do great works for God. What I appreciated most about the words that I read that day was the fact that the Holy Spirit of God had His rightful place, delivering words directly into my heart, soul, and mind. I left that meeting feeling uplifted and empowered, knowing that God had spoken to me through a book, through a man who was fulfilling God's purpose for his own life.

I went on to start the ministry that God had placed in my heart. Seven Days of Worship Christian Ministry is up and operating under the anointing of the Holy Spirit. I serve this ministry as pastor with confidence, knowing that God is with me. All that I do is done unto God for the purpose of God.

I don't doubt that I would have proceeded with this ministry without reading the introduction to this book, but certainly reading the introduction made starting our ministry much easier.

I was later granted the opportunity to read the entire book. Strong biblical facts made the message much easier to receive from the beginning of my reading.

This book answered so many questions while encouraging me to know that, no matter what anyone else thought, God is with me and that He has chosen me. It never ceases to amaze me that when discouragement comes, God always has a ram in the bush. In this case, the ram in the bush was this book. At a time when a test began to challenge what God was doing through me or to challenge the ministry itself, my good friend Ron Momon called and asked me to read this book. It came at a time when I was praying for more strength and courage to continue walking in my calling without noticing what people had to say against it.

I'm sure that those of you who have stepped out on faith and are walking in faith know what I'm talking about. There are times when Satan will rise up in people for the sole purpose of fighting God's plan for you.

I began reading, and by the time I finished the first chapter, I was good to go. I had been encouraged to walk in greater confidence, knowing that the Lord was with me and that no weapon formed against me could ever prosper. Nevertheless, I continued to read, only to feel more and more empowered. The more I read, the more I saw God's plan for my life. The more I read, the more I was influenced to remember that certain events would not have happened during my calling if God had not set them in motion.

After completing this book, I would like to sum it up this way. It's mostly biblically based. The message was clearly from God to encourage those of us chosen for last-day ministry. While reading, I knew very well that this book was not man's idea. The way it spoke to me added fuel to the fire of willingness burning inside me, clearly indicating that God was speaking to encourage His purpose for me.

Lastly, this book refers to facts from the Bible that were recorded specifically for the purpose of reminding those called by God not to look too closely at the way certain events happen while obeying God's will. We must know that we are chosen by God. God will in turn prove that He has chosen you. As it is written in Isaiah 55:8 (KJV), "For my thoughts are not your thoughts, neither are your ways my ways, saith the Lord." That's what this book emphasizes over all: the importance of being qualified by God, not by man.

Read, enjoy, and go forward. Remain in the will of God while being all God allows you to be. Thank you, Ron Momon, for obeying God and writing this book. May God bless you, and I look forward to reading more of what God has to give you in the future. Thank you.

—Pastor Jeff Thomas

Introduction

I would like to start this book off with a question to the readers. Have you ever noticed that most of the people in the Bible whom God used were not perfect? Quite the contrary. God used a man who stuttered to deliver millions, a man rejected and hated by his brothers to deliver a nation, a murderer and adulterer who was referred to as a "man after God's own heart," a fearful man to lead an army, and countless others whom you will discover in this book. Did some of those descriptions sound foolish? If you answered *yes*, then you have the right book in your hand.

Just know that God can use you right where you are presently. Don't look at your weaknesses or past failures. God is strong where you are weak!

First Corinthians 1:26–29 explains this focus in detail. This is the fundamental scripture for the writing of this book. We will look at several different translations of this scripture to give you a complete understanding.

> Brothers, think of what you were when you were called. Not many of you were wise by human standards; not many were influential; not many were of noble birth. But God chose the foolish things of the world to shame the wise; God chose the weak things of the world to shame the strong. He chose the lowly things of this world and the

despised things—and the things that are not—to nullify the things that are, so that no one may boast before him.

—1 Corinthians 1:26–29 (NIV)

Remember, dear brothers and sisters, that few of you were wise in the world's eyes, or powerful, or wealthy when God called you. Instead, God deliberately chose things the world considers foolish in order to shame those who think they are wise. And he chose those who are powerless to shame those who are powerful. God chose things despised by the world; things counted as nothing at all, and used them to bring to nothing what the world considers important, so that no one can ever boast in the presence of God.

—1 Corinthians 1:26–29 (NLT)

For [simply] consider your own call, brethren; not many [of you were considered to be] wise according to human estimates and standards, not many influential and powerful, not many of high and noble birth. [No] for God selected (deliberately chose) what in the world is foolish to put the wise to shame, and what the world calls weak to put the strong to shame. And God also selected (deliberately chose) what in the world is lowborn and insignificant and branded and treated with contempt, even the things that are nothing, that He might depose and bring to nothing the things that are, So that no mortal man should [have pretense for glorying and] boast in the presence of God.

—1 Corinthians 1:26–29 (AMP)

Take a good look, friends, at who you were when
you were called into this life. I don't see many of
"the brightest and the best" among you, not many
influential, not many from high-society families.
Isn't it obvious that God deliberately chose men
and women that the culture overlooks and exploits
and abuses chose these "nobodies" to expose the
hollow pretensions of the "somebodies?" That
makes it quite clear that none of you can get
by with blowing your own horn before God.
Everything that we have—right thinking and
right living, a clean slate and a fresh start—comes
from God by way of Jesus Christ. That's why we
have the saying, "If you're going to blow a horn,
blow a trumpet for God."
—1 Corinthians 1:26–29 (MSG)

Do you feel weak, powerless, despised, lowly, overlooked, or
merely too messed up for God to use? I don't see anyone God
used throughout the Bible who had it all together. I believe God
sees an opportunity to get more glory out of the situation by
turning around a person who is messed up or insignificant. I like
to say it like this: God likes looking for the ram in the bush or the
underdog. Have you ever noticed that people like to cheer for the
underdog? Now it's time to put on your seat belt because we are
going on a little journey to examine the lives of some of the men
and women of the Bible.

Joseph—
Rejected

Joseph was the son of Jacob and lived in the land of Canaan. Joseph was seventeen at this time. We find Joseph feeding a flock of sheep with his brothers. Joseph was a shepherd. Joseph's work as a shepherd would help him in his future calling. Don't think it's an accident to be in your current job. Israel, Joseph's father, loved him more than all his other children because he was the youngest. Joseph's brothers saw that their father loved him more. His brothers hated him and could not speak peaceably to him. Imagine having all your siblings hate you. Joseph was probably happy that his father loved him, but he was obviously hurt that his brothers hated him.

Joseph had a dream, which he told to his brothers, and they hated him even more. The dream showed Joseph and his brothers binding sheaves in a field. A sheaf is a bundle of grain. In the dream, Joseph's sheaves arose and stood upright, and his brother's sheaves stood all around and bowed down to his sheaf. Joseph's brothers were offended after the explanation of the dream. The brothers wanted to know if Joseph would rule over them. So they hated Joseph even more for his dreams and his words. Joseph had another dream and told his brothers about it, though one would think Joseph might have learned from the first time. Joseph told them that his latest dream showed the sun, the moon, and the eleven stars bowing to him. Joseph told his brothers and his father about the dream. Joseph's father, Israel, expressed his disapproval and wondered about this most recent dream. Israel wanted to know if Joseph's family would bow down to the earth before him. Israel took offense at this. Joseph's brothers envied him. God was showing Joseph his future in these dreams. We will get into that later. Joseph was young and probably didn't know any better. The explanation of these dreams made Joseph look prideful and arrogant on the surface. This is a reason you have to use wisdom when sharing knowledge with people. Just because God told you something doesn't mean that you should tell anyone about it. It's best to make sure, first of all, that the person knows your heart. Secondly, pray to make sure the timing is right.

Joseph went out one day to find his brothers in the field feeding the flock. When his brothers saw Joseph approaching, they conspired to kill him.

If you fail to deal with anger, jealousy, and resentment, they could lead you to do some bad deeds. Those feelings will leave the door open for Satan to come in. Sometimes people misinterpret what you tell them. Imagine your father favoring a sibling over you, and then imagine that person telling you he or she will rule over you someday. I think most people would take that the wrong way.

The brothers conspired to kill Joseph and cast him into a pit. The brothers plotted to tell their father that a wild animal had devoured Joseph. One of the brothers, Reuben, heard the other brothers conspiring, and he was able to talk them out of killing Joseph.

Instead of killing Joseph, Reuben wanted to put Joseph in a pit without any bloodshed. Reuben plotted to rescue Joseph and take him home. The brothers took Joseph and threw him into the pit. The brothers saw a group of Ishmaelite traders coming from Gilead with their camels on their way to Egypt. Can you say *divine appointment*? Judah, another of Joseph's brothers, also thought it was a bad idea to kill Joseph. Judah suggested that they sell Joseph to the Ishmaelites. The other brothers agreed and sold Joseph for twenty shekels of silver (equivalent to about $230). That must have been some serious animosity the brothers had for them to sell Joseph into slavery. The Ishmaelites bought Joseph and took him to Egypt.

Joseph's brothers took one of his garments and dipped it in goat's blood to give the appearance that he had been killed. The brothers took the garment to Joseph's father, Israel, and told him they had found it. Israel tore his clothes, put sackcloth on his waist (a sign of mourning), and mourned for many days. The Ishmaelites sold Joseph in Egypt to a man named Potiphar. Potiphar was an officer of the Egyptian ruler, the pharaoh, and captain of the guard. We will see later that this outcome was also a divine appointment. When I say *divine appointment*, I simply mean that events do not occur by chance. God allows certain outcomes to get us into a place where He wants us to be. A good friend of mine, Tim Burell, uses that phrase all the time. I know he won't mind me using it. Nothing just happens, Tim.

Don't think it's an accident that you chose your particular profession when you chose it. God put the desire in your heart. So stop questioning your decision to go into that particular job. Nothing just happens.

So Potiphar bought Joseph and took him to be a servant in his home. Genesis 39:2 shows us something very interesting. The Lord was with Joseph, and he was a successful man. And he was in the house of his master, the Egyptian. Another translation of this scripture uses the word *prosperous* instead of *successful*.

The original Hebrew word for *prosperous* is *tsalach*, which means *to advance, prosper, make progress, succeed,* or *be profitable.* When studying the Bible, it's best to look up certain words in their original language for better understanding. Let's talk about Joseph's status for a minute. How could Joseph be successful or prosperous if he was a slave at the time? Interesting question, isn't it? I will tell you how Joseph was successful. The scripture says the Lord was with Joseph; therefore, he was a successful man. You see, no matter what physical state you are currently in, if the Lord is with you, you are successful. We tend to look at the material goods a person has to make a determination about whether he or she is successful or not. Well, my friend, God doesn't look at it the same way. Don't misunderstand me. There is nothing wrong with material possessions as long as they don't come before God. If the Lord is with you, however, you are successful, however you may appear on the surface. Success is first becoming mentally strong before anything manifests materially. If you know who you are in God, it is just a matter of time before the inward manifests into the outward. I don't have time to get into this progression in detail in this book, but I will give you two scriptures for meditation.

"This Book of the Law shall not depart from your mouth, but you shall meditate on it day and night, that you may observe to do according to all that is written in it. For then you will make your way prosperous, and then you will have good success," as it is written in Joshua 1:8.

"Beloved, I pray that you may prosper in all things and be in health, just as your soul prospers," as it is written in 3 John 1:2.

The soul is your mind, will, and emotions. There is a direct correlation between the way you think and success. If you take the time to read stories about wealthy or successful people, you will always see a successful mentality or way of thinking. If you meditate on the word of God day and night, as it states in the book of Joshua, you will have good success.

There is something about God's word that will propel you and bring success. Business ideas will come, inventions will come, and concepts will come. Just don't let the success take God out of first place in your life.

Let's get back to Joseph. Joseph's master, Potiphar, saw that the Lord was with Joseph and that the Lord made all he did prosper in his hand. So Joseph found favor in Potiphar's sight, and Potiphar made him overseer of his house.

Potiphar put everything under Joseph's authority. It wasn't long before Potiphar saw that everything around Joseph began to prosper. Potiphar knew this was because the blessing of the Lord was on Joseph. Wouldn't that get someone's attention? What if a person knew you were a believer, and then he or she began to prosper because the Lord was with you? "I will bless those who bless you," as it is expressed in Genesis 12:3. If people saw such blessings, they would eventually want to hear about this God you believe in. If for no other reason, curiosity would be enough. This is your open door to talk to others about the Lord. This doesn't mean that you beat them over the head with the Bible. Start off by sharing your personal testimony of how you found the Lord. You will be amazed where the conversation goes from there.

I hope you know that just because everything is going well doesn't mean that Satan will just go away. Potiphar's wife began to show interest in Joseph. The wife began to ask Joseph to sleep with her. Joseph refused all her advances. Joseph told her that this would be sinning against God. Maybe if we would think of sin like Joseph did, it would minimize sin in our own lives. Potiphar's wife caught Joseph alone in the house one particular day and asked him again to sleep with her. Joseph refused her advances again. She grabbed Joseph by his shirt, and Joseph ran away to the outside of the house—leaving the shirt in her hand. The worldly mentality would say, "Why is he running away from this opportunity?" But the godly mentality would say, "Good job, Joseph, for resisting sin." The word of God tells us in several places to flee from these things. In 1 Corinthians 6:18, we are told to "flee sexual immorality." When Potiphar's wife saw that Joseph had left his garment in her hand and fled outside, she tried to insult him by telling the men of her house that Joseph had tried to sleep with her. Potiphar was angered by this news from his wife. Potiphar took Joseph and put him in prison.

Joseph was wrongfully accused and thrown into prison. Can you say, "God isn't finished yet"? The Lord was with Joseph and showed him mercy while he was in prison. Joseph was given favor in the sight of the keeper of the prison. The keeper put Joseph in charge of all the prisoners. The keeper of the prison saw that the Lord was with Joseph, and whatever he did, the Lord made it prosper. Can you see a pattern here? Whatever the situation or circumstance, the Lord can show you favor and change it. Nothing is impossible if you are serving God Almighty! What amazes me the most about Joseph is that he did not complain. Joseph could have been negative and talked about all the bad events that kept occurring. I believe these situations were building character in Joseph.

Let's pick up with the pharaoh, the king of Egypt. The pharaoh became angry with his two officers, the chief butler and the chief baker, and put them into the prison. Joseph just happened to be in the same prison. Can you say *divine appointment*? Nothing just happens by coincidence. The captain of the guard placed Joseph in charge of the chief butler and chief baker. Joseph served them as they were in custody for a while. Then the butler and the baker had a dream. Both of them had a dream in the same night. Each dream had its own interpretation. Joseph came in to see them in the morning, looked at them, and saw that they were sad. Joseph wanted to know why they were sad.

They told Joseph that they had both had dreams but had no interpreter. Joseph told them that interpretations belong to God. The chief butler told his dream to Joseph, and Joseph was able to interpret the dream. Through the interpretation, Joseph told the butler that the pharaoh would restore him in three days. Joseph asked the butler to remember him when the pharaoh restored him. Joseph told him to make mention to the pharaoh so he could be freed from the prison. Now the chief baker told Joseph about his dream. Joseph interpreted the dream, telling him that the pharaoh would hang him within three days. All these events that Joseph predicted occurred. The chief butler was restored to his position but did not remember Joseph.

Two years later, the pharaoh had a dream in which he stood by the river. In the dream, the pharaoh saw seven cows, healthy and fat, coming out of the river and feeding in the meadow. Then seven other cows, ugly and thin, came out of the river and stood by the other cows on the bank of the river. The ugly, thin cows ate up the healthy, fat cows. The pharaoh woke up from his dream, slept again, and dreamed a second time. In this dream, seven heads of grain came up on one stalk, plump and good. Then seven thin heads, ruined by the east wind, sprang up after them. The seven thin heads devoured the seven plump and full heads. He woke, troubled by these dreams, and sent for the magicians of Egypt and all its wise men. The pharaoh told them his dreams, but there was no one who could interpret them. The chief butler then remembered Joseph. See, it's all about God's timing and not our own. Maybe patience is what you are lacking, my friend. The chief butler told the pharaoh about Joseph and how he had interpreted his dream and the chief baker's dream. The butler told the pharaoh that Joseph's interpretation of their dreams had proven accurate.

The pharaoh sent for Joseph, and they brought him quickly out of the jail. Joseph shaved, changed his clothing, and came to the pharaoh, who told Joseph that he had a dream, but no one was able to interpret it; he had heard about Joseph's interpretation of dreams. Quickly and in humility, Joseph gave the glory to God and got the focus off himself. Remember, folks, it's never about us. Humility is a prerequisite for God to use you for His glory. The pharaoh told Joseph about the dream. Joseph told the pharaoh that the two dreams were one and that God had shown what He was about to do. The seven good cows and seven good heads represented seven years.

Likewise, the seven thin and ugly cows and the seven empty heads ruined by the east wind were seven years of famine. Joseph said that seven years of great plenty would come throughout Egypt; then seven years of famine would deplete the land. The plenty will not be known in the land because of the famine following, for it will be very severe. Joseph told the pharaoh that God would soon bring the events of this dream to pass.

Joseph told the pharaoh that he needed to select a discerning and wise man and set him over the land of Egypt. Did you notice that Joseph didn't offer to take the job? Joseph also instructed the pharaoh to appoint officers to collect a fifth of the produce during the seven plentiful years. Joseph told the pharaoh to let them gather all the food of those good years and store up grain under the authority of the pharaoh to keep food in the cities. Then that food would serve as a reserve for the land for the seven years of famine to prevent mass starvation. So the advice of Joseph was good in the eyes of the pharaoh and his servants. The ruler saw the Spirit of God on Joseph's life. We have seen, time and time again, that even evil men can see if the Lord is operating in a person's life. The pharaoh couldn't think of anyone more discerning and wise than Joseph and appointed Joseph as steward over his house, and all his people. Joseph became the second-in-command over all of Egypt.

If we are faithful in small matters, God will eventually promote us to bigger ones. God knows how to promote people at the right time.

The pharaoh took a signet ring off his hand and put it on Joseph's hand, clothed him in garments of fine linen, and put a gold chain around his neck. We will refer back to this signet ring in a moment. The pharaoh had Joseph ride in the second chariot and set Joseph over all the land of Egypt. The pharaoh also told Joseph that no man would be able to lift his hand or foot in all the land of Egypt without Joseph's consent. The pharaoh called Joseph *Zaphnath-Paaneah*. *Zaphnath-Paaneah* means "God Speaks and He Lives." So Joseph went out over all the land of Egypt. Joseph was thirty years old at this time.

Now we are starting to see the physical manifestation of what we saw back in Genesis 39:2; the Lord was with Joseph, and he was a successful man. Joseph was destined to be in Egypt at this particular time.

God allowed Joseph to be sold into slavery to arrive at his ultimate destination. Let's examine some of the items given to Joseph by the pharaoh. The ruler gave Joseph some items as tokens of authority. The first item given to Joseph was a signet ring. During those days, a signet ring was used to designate authority, honor, or ownership. The pharaoh was simply showing that he has given Joseph authority throughout the land of Egypt. Joseph was now the most important person in all of Egypt after its ruler. Anyone seeing Joseph wearing the pharaoh's ring would automatically know he had been given authority. If you are a believer in Jesus, then you have been given authority. The name of Jesus is our signet ring. "And these signs shall follow them that believe; *In my name* shall they cast out devils; they shall speak with new tongues; They shall take up serpents; and if they drink any deadly thing, it shall not hurt them; they shall lay hands on the sick, and they shall recover," according to Mark 16:18 (italics mine).

The next items the pharaoh gave Joseph were garments of fine linen. These garments signified wealth. Another amazing aspect of this gift is that Joseph was an Israelite. Don't tell me God can't do amazing things. To the people of those times, giving an Israelite this much authority and power in Egypt would be considered foolish. The Israelites were slaves all over Egypt at the time. Joseph was thirty years old when he stood before the pharaoh in this position. That's foolish also. During those times, positions of power were typically given through family lineage only. One other thing to note is that Joseph was raised a shepherd. No one would have believed that a shepherd boy would grow up to be the second-in-command of Egypt. Shepherds would be considered lowly. God likes to confuse the wise by using the "foolish things." Wise people without God tend to think they have all the answers.

Joseph immediately went throughout the land and began to gather up all the surplus food of the seven plentiful years. Joseph stored the food throughout the land. Joseph gathered up immeasurable quantities of grain.

Then the seven years of plenty ended, and the seven years of famine began, as Joseph had said. The famine was in all the surrounding lands, but in the land of Egypt, there was bread. So when the Egyptians were famished, the people cried to the pharaoh for bread. He told the Egyptians to go to Joseph. The ruler also told them to do whatever Joseph told them to do. The famine was over all the face of the earth, and Joseph opened all the storehouses and sold grain to the Egyptians. Even so, the famine became severe in the land of Egypt. All the surrounding countries came to Joseph in Egypt to buy grain because of the famine. Now we will see Joseph's family come back into the picture.

When Israel (Joseph's father) saw that there was grain in Egypt, he sent his sons down to Egypt to buy grain. These are the same brothers who had sold Joseph into slavery. Israel didn't let Benjamin go to Egypt with his other brothers. The brothers arrived in Egypt. The brothers came and bowed down before Joseph with their faces to the earth. This was a fulfillment of the dream Joseph had prior to being sold into slavery. Joseph saw his brothers and recognized them, but he acted as a stranger to them and spoke roughly to them. The brothers didn't recognize Joseph.

Joseph remembered the dreams that he had about his brothers. The brothers explained to Joseph that they were there to buy food. Joseph told them that he thought they were spies. Joseph told them to bring their youngest brother so he would be convinced they were not spies. Joseph did this to trick his brothers into bringing Benjamin, his youngest brother.

His brothers went home and reluctantly returned with Benjamin. Joseph saw his brother Benjamin approaching him with the other brothers. Joseph walked away for a short time to weep. Joseph washed his face and returned a short time later. Joseph told his servants to serve bread. So they set him a place by himself, and his brothers a place by themselves, and the Egyptians who ate with him by themselves. This was because the Egyptians could not eat food with the Israelites, for that would be an abomination to the Egyptians. Let's discuss this for a moment. This should help you see how Joseph's appointment was foolish in the eyes of the world. The Egyptians thought it was an abomination even to eat food with the Hebrews. God made Joseph second-in-command in Egypt amongst people who didn't even want to eat with Hebrews. All things are possible with God. Don't let the boundaries set by man convince you that God can't use you. God has proven time and time again that he likes to go against the norms of society.

Joseph had his servants put his silver cup in the sack of Benjamin prior to their leaving. Joseph did this to set them up. Joseph sent his servants to go after the brothers when they departed. The servants stopped them and told them the man who carried the silver cup would be Joseph's slave. Benjamin returned to become Joseph's slave. This decree was a way to get Joseph's father to come to Egypt. Joseph couldn't restrain himself anymore and put all the servants out of the room as he revealed to his brothers his true identity. His brothers were astonished as Joseph revealed himself. Joseph told them to not be grieved or angry with themselves because he was sold into slavery. Joseph told them that God sent him before them in Egypt to preserve life. Joseph also told them that it was God who sent him to the pharaoh to be a lord of his entire house and a ruler throughout all the land of Egypt. The brothers went to get their father and brought him to Egypt to be reunited with Joseph. The entire family came to Egypt. Joseph informed the pharaoh that his family was in Egypt now. The ruler came to meet the family of Joseph. Joseph's family told him that they came to live in Egypt because the famine was severe in their land.

The pharaoh told Joseph to have his family live in Goshen, the best area. I often wonder what would have happened if the family had not wished to settle there.

There are some people who think Christians should never have the best. As I stated earlier, God doesn't care if we have nice things as long as those things don't have us, though I don't have time to get into that topic. That would be for another book. Well, this move to the best land in Goshen would prove important during the time of Moses.

As I have mentioned previously, every event has a purpose for God—God's purpose, not individuals' purposes. Keeping God first keeps us out of trouble. What a story. Think about some of the trials you have been through in your life. We spend so much time complaining about different things that occur in our lives. Joseph never complained one time. Joseph was rejected by his own brothers, falsely accused, thrown in jail for no reason, and mistreated. Do you know there is a reason for everything we go through in life?

> For no temptation (no trial regarded as enticing to sin), [no matter how it comes or where it leads] has overtaken you and laid hold on you that is not common to man [that is, no temptation or trial has come to you that is beyond human resistance and that is not adjusted and adapted and belonging to human experience, and such as man can bear]. But God is faithful [to His Word and to His compassionate nature], and He [can be trusted] not to let you be tempted and tried and assayed beyond your ability and strength of resistance and power to endure, but with the temptation He

will [always] also provide the way out (the means of escape to a landing place), that you may be capable and strong and powerful to bear up under it patiently.

(1 Corinthians 10:13 AMP)

This is one of my favorite scriptures. Just think about it for a moment; God will not allow us to be tempted or tried beyond our ability to handle it. So if you are going through adversity currently, God has said that you can make it through, or you would not be going through it. How are you going to have a testimony if you never go through any tests? Did you notice that the word *testimony* has *test* in it? So don't concentrate on the negative; concentrate on God and know that He is in control, no matter what it looks like.

2

Moses—
a Speech Impediment and Anger

Now let's take a look at the life of Moses. The life of Moses began with turmoil. The Hebrew midwives were given instructions by the pharaoh, the king of Egypt, to kill any Hebrew male child born. Moses was hidden by his mother after his birth. She eventually put Moses in a basket and placed him on the river. As only God would have it, the daughter of the pharaoh discovered baby Moses in the basket. She decided to keep Moses and take care of him. She raised Moses to adulthood. This is a perfect example of shaming the wise, as our foundational scripture states in 1 Corinthians. So let's think about this for a minute. Moses was raised from infancy in the pharaoh's house even though he was a Hebrew. He was living in the same household of the very person who wanted all male Hebrew babies killed. God uses the foolish things to confuse the wise! There is no man who can interfere with the plan of God. That sentence deserves repetition. There is no man who can interfere with the plan of God. This is what I call the favor of God.

One day Moses observed a fellow Hebrew being beaten by an Egyptian. Moses killed the Egyptian and hid him in the sand.

Moses went out the next day and observed two Hebrew men fighting. He began to question the two men about their dispute. One of the men wanted to know who made Moses a prince and a judge over them. The men reminded Moses that he had killed an Egyptian. Moses immediately feared that it was known that he had murdered an Egyptian. The pharaoh learned of the killing and sought to kill Moses. Moses fled from Egypt to Midian. This particular pharaoh eventually died over the course of time. The children of Israel cried out to God because of their continued bondage to Egypt. God heard their cries and remembered His covenant with Abraham, Isaac, and Jacob. This reminds me of the great Psalm 112 that tells us a righteous man is in everlasting remembrance of the covenant that God established with Abraham. And Galatians 3 tells us that if you are in Christ, you are heirs according to this covenant.

So we are also to remember the covenant. That is a subject for another book, so we will move on. Let's get back to Moses. Moses fled to the city of Midian and took up residence with Jethro, the priest of Midian. It is rather significant that Moses would take up residence with a priest. Moses would become a priest in the very near future. The experience of working with Jethro would help him tremendously in the future. Remember, Moses had killed a man previously in Egypt, so he had to flee to another place. Jethro began to favor Moses and gave his daughter Zipporah to Moses in marriage. Moses took care of the flock of Jethro, his father-in-law, in the back of the desert. Thus God prepared Moses to take care of the flock of God in the future. As I stated previously, nothing we do in life is by accident. Don't ever think your current assignment is a mistake. Of course, at this time, Moses didn't know that someday he would lead the flock of God out of Egypt. You may be at a point in your life where you don't realize the full plan God has for your life. You may ask yourself, "How do I find the plan for my life?" I have one simple answer for you. Seek God continuously through prayer for the plan until it is revealed to you. God will reveal to you the specific plan for your life. God has shown us, in His word, several different ways the plan may be revealed. God has revealed the plan through dreams, visions, and the still, small voice of the Holy Spirit. Remember the dreams that God gave Joseph. Those dreams showed Joseph the plan God had for his life. God has also used prophets, fellow Christians, and many other ways to reveal His plan. The Old Testament has plenty of examples of prophets revealing God's plan. This list is inconclusive because we can't place God in a box. Remember He is God Almighty all by Himself. Once you have an idea of the plan, get ready. Don't use the excuse that you don't have the entire plan. God will lead you down the pathway to your destination. Remember, "Nothing just happens."

Let's resume the story of Moses, who was then tending Jethro's sheep. He would soon tend the sheep of God. Now it was time for God to reveal Himself to Moses. God appeared to Moses in the desert out of a burning bush. God began to tell Moses that He had seen the oppression of His people in Egypt and had heard their cry. God intended Moses to deliver the children of Israel from Egypt. God revealed this plan to Moses in the desert. Moses asked God an interesting question in the book of Exodus. In Exodus 3:11, we read, "But Moses said to God, 'Who am I that I should go unto Pharaoh, and that I should bring forth the children of Israel out of Egypt?'" This is a question that most of us ask God from time to time: "Who am I?" Which side of the fence you grew up on, your flaws, your educational background, your reputation, and your self-image do not matter; you are somebody in the eyes of God. God has a plan to use you for His will! Yes, you, the person reading this book. Let's get back to Moses. God promised Moses that He would be with him every step of the way. Moses continued to look for a way out of the call of God on his life. In Exodus 3:13–14, Moses asked God another question.

"And Moses said unto God, behold, when I come to the children of Israel, and say to them, The God of your fathers has sent me to you; and they shall say to me, what is his name? What shall I say to them? And God said to Moses, I AM that I AM: and he said, thus shall you say to the children of Israel, I AM has sent me to you."

What is your excuse for God not being able to use you? God already has the answer. Moses didn't know, but God had already laid out the pathway for him. If God calls you to do something for Him, He will equip you for the task. If God has given you a vision, He will equip you for it. This is called *provision*. One definition of *provision* is *providing for a particular matter*. In other words, whatever God has called you to do, he will provide the resources for you to fulfill it. Stop looking at what you have in the bank account. Remember God called you to do this. Don't ever forget it. Remembering this will help keep you grounded.

You will begin to see several similarities between some of the men and women in this book. Most of them went through some type of trial or tribulation. Some of them experienced rejection also. After they endured the test or trial, the reward was waiting for them on the other side. I'm referring to the reward of provision.

Moses went back and forth with God a few times before finally accepting the call. Moses finally realized that God could use him. Yes, God can use a person who has made many mistakes previously in his life, including killing another man. Isn't that foolish to the world? How can God use a murderer? A murderer is no different from you and me except that the murderer made a mistake. Don't we all make mistakes?

In Isaiah 55:8–9, we read, "'For My thoughts are not your thoughts; nor are your ways My ways,' says the Lord. 'For as the heavens are higher than the earth, so are My ways higher than your ways, and My thoughts than your thoughts.'"

Next we see God begin to reveal the plan of action to Moses. There are many people who have been given the plan, but they refuse to act. You have to add some action to your faith. We all must realize that God will show us what to do. You are not in this alone. God is the one who called you to action. I had to remind myself of this while writing this book. I have previously told God that He told me to write this book, so I'm not going to stress. You should have the same attitude when things start to get tough as you move into the specific plan God gave you. Remind God that He gave you the vision so you will rest easily at night. Say this: "God, my Father, you gave this to me, so I'm up for the challenge." Say it a second time. Say it as many times as necessary to rid yourself of the stress.

Moses allowed doubt to creep into his head again.

> Then Moses said, "But suppose they will not believe me or listen to my voice; suppose they say, 'The Lord has not appeared to you.' So the Lord said to him, 'What is that in your hand?' He said, 'A rod.' And He said, 'Cast it on the ground.' So he cast it on the ground, and it became a serpent; and Moses fled from it. Then the Lord said to Moses, 'Reach out your hand and take it by the tail' (and he reached out his hand and caught it, and it became a rod in his hand), 'that they may believe that the Lord God of their fathers, the God of Abraham,the God of Isaac, and the God of Jacob, has appeared to you.'" (Exodus 4:1–5, NKJV)

What is in your hand? Think about that for a moment. If you answered, "Nothing," you are just where God wants you. The very thing(s) around you are what God can use to manifest His power through you. You receive your talents, skills, and possessions from God for God's purposes rather than your own. God can use what may seem insignificant to you for His glory.

Moses had yet another excuse. That excuse is discussed in Exodus 4:11–12: "Then Moses said to the Lord, 'O my Lord, I am not eloquent, neither before nor since you have spoken to your servant; but I am slow of speech and slow of tongue.'"

"So the Lord said to him, 'Who has made man's mouth? Or who makes the mute, the deaf, the seeing, or the blind? Have not I, the Lord? Now therefore, go, and I will be with your mouth and teach you what you shall say.'"

Remember, God is the manufacturer. He knows everything about you: past, present, and future. What better place to have a Mercedes Benz repaired than a Mercedes ® Service Center? The technicians there know that car inside and out because Mercedes Benz manufactured it. Likewise, God knows you inside and out. Just trust Him. Moses continued to make excuses to the Lord. Finally the Lord became angry with Moses. Moses was not satisfied that God would be his mouthpiece. Moses asked God to send someone else. The Lord sent Aaron to assist Moses and to be his spokesman. Aaron was the brother of Moses. Aaron was the solution to the reservations that Moses had about public speaking. God knows how to take away all your excuses. Doubt, unbelief, and condemnation lead to excuses. I have an entire chapter dedicated to guilt, shame, and condemnation.

Doubt, unbelief, and condemnation take place in the battleground of the mind. What do I mean by *the battleground of the mind*? I'm glad you asked. It's a battleground because thoughts dominate our minds. The good thoughts are battling with the bad thoughts that Satan plants in the mind. It's really a matter of how many of the things of God you are putting in versus how many of the things of Satan. Satan loves to plant doubt, unbelief, and condemnation in your mind. We will refer to Satan from now on as "the enemy." The enemy wants you to believe that you are not gifted enough, you don't speak well enough, or that you have many other flaws according to the world's standards. Well, fortunately, God doesn't operate by the world's standards.

This is the reason God told Moses, "I AM." God is whatever you need Him to be. God further illustrated this by revealing different characteristics of His name. God revealed Himself as Jehovah Jireh, "Your Provision," Jehovah Rophe, "Your Healer," Jehovah Tsidkenu, "Your Righteousness," Jehovah Shalom, "Your Peace," Jehovah Rohi, "Your Shepherd," and many more. God wants you to fill in the blank " I AM ____.

Now Moses was ready to begin walking in the call of God. Moses went to his father-in-law Jethro to ask his permission to leave. Jethro gave Moses his permission to leave. God is all about authority. God didn't tell Moses to leave until after Jethro gave his permission. The book of Romans tells us that there is no authority except from God, and the authorities that exist are appointed by God. Therefore, whoever resists the authority resists the ordinance of God, and those who resist will bring judgment on themselves, according to Romans 13:1–2.

Moses displayed proper submission to divine authority by asking his permission to leave. This is one reason why some people struggle. They are resisting the authority God placed in their lives. Are you resisting your parents? Are you resisting the laws and ordinances of your local or state municipality? I hope you answered *no*. If not, repent and get it fixed. People are resisting the authorities of government, parents, or whatever other authority God has placed in their lives. Make it easier on yourself; stop resisting the authority in your life! God has also instructed us to pray for the authorities he has placed in our lives. God told Moses it was now safe for him to return to Egypt. Moses left Midian, taking his wife and his sons to Egypt.

Moses also took the staff of God in his hand, which signified authority and provision. God told Moses to do wonders with the staff before the pharaoh. God warned Moses that He would harden the heart of the pharaoh so that he would not let the people go. In other words, God was going to cause the pharaoh to be stubborn. Nothing just happens. We will see later how God was able to get glory out of the pharaoh's hardened heart. You see, there is a reason why that person is acting that way toward you.

God gave Moses the final instructions before he would face off against the pharaoh for the first time. The time to see the pharaoh finally arrived. Moses and Aaron went to him and told him the Lord God of Israel had said, "Let my people go!" The pharaoh told Moses he did not know this Lord and would not let the people go. They continued to plead. Instead of releasing them, the ruler increased the workload of the Hebrew slaves. The slaves were also beaten. The people blamed Moses for their increased workload. You can't let people discourage you from doing what God calls you to do even when these people are the very people you are trying to help.

God began to tell Moses what He would do to the pharaoh and that the pharaoh would drive the Hebrews out of his land. God went on further to tell Moses that He revealed Himself to his ancestors (Abraham, Isaac, and Jacob) as God Almighty (El Shaddai). God told Moses that they didn't know Him as Lord. *Lord* means *Yahweh* or *Jehovah.* This is the redemptive name of God, or the aspect of His nature that would bring His people out of bondage.

God told Moses to go back to His people in Egypt and tell them that He would free them from bondage to Egypt and redeem them. Moses went to tell the children of Israel what God had said. They would not listen to Moses. This response reminds me of the reactions of many today when true men of God bring instructions from the Lord. Moses knew what God told him, so he was not discouraged even though the people would not listen.

The enemy will use people to bring doubt and unbelief. This is why it's important to know the direction in which God is leading you. God told Moses to tell the pharaoh for the second time to let His people go. Moses told God that the children of Israel would not listen, so why should the pharaoh listen? Here we see some of the insecurities and doubts trying to rise up. The enemy will use these opportunities to plant doubt and unbelief in your mind.

When you begin to look at your own abilities, you will fail every time. Say out loud, "It's not about me!" God wants you to trust Him totally. He knows the vision He gave you is too big for you. Can you say, "Nothing is too hard for God!"? One of my favorite scriptures in the Bible is Matthew 19:26, which states, "With men this is impossible, but with God all things are possible." So when obstacles to the vision that God has given you are staring you in the face, just remember, nothing is impossible with God!

God sent Moses and Aaron to speak to the pharaoh on seven different occasions. You may ask, "Why seven?" I'm glad you asked that question. God is very purposeful in everything He does. The number seven means divine completion and perfection. God created the earth in seven days. Everything was perfect after those seven days. In Joshua 6, the number seven was again significant. According to the biblical account, after the Israelites marched around the city of Jericho once a day for six days, on the seventh day, they encircled the city seven times. On the seventh time around, the priests blew the trumpets, the people shouted, and the walls of the city fell flat. I could retell more stories in the Bible related to the number seven. Just know that God chose for Moses and Aaron to go before the pharaoh seven times for his specific purpose of divine perfection and completeness. The pharaoh finally released the children of Israel into the care of Moses after ten different plagues came upon the nation. Let's consider these plagues for a moment. The first plague caused the water to become blood, which killed all the fish and left no drinking water. The second plague caused frogs to come forth out of the river and take over the entire land. The third plague was an infestation of lice throughout Egypt. The fourth plague was a swarm of flies throughout the nation. There was no swarm of flies in the land of Goshen where the children of Israel lived.

Remember back in Chapter 1, where Joseph's family was settled in Goshen? Remember, I wrote that God wanted them in Goshen for a specific purpose. It was all about God's provision for His people. God knows how to get you to a certain place to receive His provision. The fifth plague was disease coming upon the livestock in the nation. All the livestock in Egypt died except the livestock that belonged to the children of Israel. The sixth plague was boils (sores) affecting humans and beasts. The seventh plague was hail in Egypt. However, there was no hail in Goshen, where the children of Israel dwelled. The eighth plague was locusts devouring all the crops. The ninth plague was darkness for three days in Egypt while the children of Israel had light in Goshen. The tenth and final plague was the death of all firstborn Egyptian children. The children of Israel didn't suffer a loss in this plague either. If you read chapters 7–11 of Exodus, you will notice that during the first three plagues, only the magicians of Egypt were able to imitate the plagues created by God through Moses. Remember one thing about the enemy: He is not a creator, but he is an imitator. The enemy also tries to pervert what God creates. It's rather like money; it can be good or bad, depending on its use. God will allow the enemy to go only so far before He will step in and turn the situation around for His glory. In Job 1, we see the enemy having to get permission from God before he does certain things. See Job 1:6–12. There is no need to be afraid of the enemy. Believe me, God knows how to keep the enemy in check.

Starting with the fourth plague, we see God's hand upon His children. You see, God wants distinction between His children and the children of the enemy. God loves you and wants to place His hand of protection over you. Romans 10:9–10 shows the only way to become a child of God. We will discuss this topic more at the end of the book. The swarm of flies came upon the entire land of Egypt except the land of Goshen.

Moses told the pharaoh in Exodus 8:22–23: "And in that day I will set apart the land of Goshen, in which My people dwell, that no swarms of flies shall be there, in order that you may know that I am the Lord in the midst of the land. I will make a difference between My people and your people."

There is no need to worry about what is going on in the world; God has you covered if you are His child. No matter who sits in the Oval Office of the White House, God is in control. The world is getting darker and darker, but it doesn't matter. If you have faith to believe that God will protect you, consider it done. Some may think that God was only a God of the Old Testament. God is the same yesterday, today, and forever. God never changes, as we read in both Malachi 3:6 and Hebrews 13:8.

In Exodus 9:4, God said he would make a distinction between the livestock of Israel and the livestock of Egypt in the fifth plague. All the livestock in Egypt died, but all the livestock of Israel lived. God has made a distinction of His children throughout the Bible. And during the final plague, all the firstborn children of the Egyptians died, but the firstborns of the Israelites were spared. So for those who think they can wipe Israel off the face of the planet, I have a simple message: "It's not going to happen!" God has his hand on the nation of Israel. Look at this tiny country (Israel) surrounded by nations that want to destroy it. Many have tried to destroy Israel but all have failed. The fact that God's hand is on the nation of Israel has been proven throughout history. All the countries that have attacked Israel have faltered in defeat. When Israel rebelled against God, He removed His hand of protection. We see examples of this throughout the Old Testament.

The United States of America has been a blessed nation because of its support of Israel. The Bible tells us that anyone blessing the nation Israel will be blessed and anyone who curses Israel will be cursed. See Genesis 12:3. Some of the worst famines and droughts in history have occurred in nations that cut off diplomatic ties to Israel. Millions of people died during these famines.

History has shown the fulfillment of this scripture. Throughout history, many empires have sent armies to capture Jerusalem. The

Jews suffered under each of them, but their empires eventually fell apart. The Egyptian, Roman, Babylonian, Persian, and Greek empires all fell, and not by accident. God said He would curse those that cursed Israel. I don't need to say any more; just look at history.

You may be thinking, "All this talk about Israel—what about me?" I'm glad you asked that question. Please allow me one tangent before we get back to Moses. In Genesis 12 we see God establishing an everlasting covenant with Abraham and his ancestors. A covenant is a pledge between two or more parties. (I know I wrote that this topic would have to wait for another book. This is too good to wait for the next book.) There were certain promises that God made to Abraham and his descendants in this covenant established with Abraham.

Abraham is considered the founding father of the nation of Israel. Galatians 3:26–29 states, "For you are all sons of God through faith in Christ Jesus. For as many of you as were baptized into Christ have put on Christ. There is neither Jew nor Greek, there is neither slave nor free, there is neither male nor female; for you are all one in Christ Jesus. And if you are Christ's, then you are Abraham's seed, and heirs according to the promise." So if you have accepted Jesus as your Lord and savior, you are Abraham's spiritual seed and an heir of the promise. So you are considered a spiritual member of the nation of Israel. Do you see the connection? This is why Israel should be dear to every Christian's heart. I wish there were more time to discuss the covenant, but that subject is so broad that it would take another book. I will touch on it again slightly toward the end of this book.

Let's get back to Moses in Exodus 13. The pharaoh finally released the people. As we read in Exodus 12:31, he summoned Moses and Aaron by night and said, "Rise, go out from among my people, both you and the children of Israel. And go serve the Lord as you have said."

Historical records note that close to one million men, women, and children marched out of Egypt toward the Red Sea by way of the wilderness. The Lord was with them as they marched through the wilderness. The Lord went before them by day in a pillar of cloud to lead the way and by night in a pillar of fire to give them light. So they knew that God was with them, day and night.

God revealed to Moses that He would harden the heart of the pharaoh one last time. God told Moses that the pharaoh would pursue them. Exodus 14:4–5 states, "Then I will harden Pharaoh's heart, so that he will pursue them; and I will gain honor over Pharaoh and over all his army, that the Egyptians may know that I am the Lord." And they did so. Now the king of Egypt was told that the people had fled, and the hearts of the pharaoh and his servants were turned against the people; and they said, "Why have we done this that we have let Israel go from serving us?"

Isn't it interesting that at this point, the pharaoh began to ask why he let them go? Just remember that God had the heart of the king in His hand and turned it wherever or however He pleased. So the pharaoh took his army and began to pursue the Israelites. The army drew closer as the Israelites approached the Red Sea. The Israelites saw the army, became afraid, and cried out to the Lord. They began to doubt Moses again. They told Moses that he had brought them into the wilderness to die. Some people just refused to see the hand of God at work. Moses told them to stand still and see the salvation of the Lord. When opposition or obstacles are staring you in the eyes, you have to look at them and begin to speak the word of God. Grab a scripture out of the Bible and put it in your mouth.

I like what Moses said in Exodus 14:13: "Stand still and see the salvation of the Lord," That scripture works for many situations. I will tell you why this scripture works. The original Hebrew meanings of *salvation* are *welfare, prosperity, deliverance,* and *victory.* So when you say, "See the salvation of the Lord," you are actually saying, "See His deliverance, see His victory," and so forth. The Bible says that life and death are in the power of the tongue. You have to make a conscious decision, before the opposition comes, that you will speak life and not death to the situation. It's amazing how, when you speak the word of God, faith begins to rise within you. Angels also begin to work on your behalf when the word of God is spoken. As it is written in Psalm 103:20, "Bless the Lord, you His angels, who excel in strength, who do His word, Heeding unto the voice of His word."

Most people know the rest of this story. God told Moses to hold the rod up in the air, and the Red Sea began to open up. The children of Israel walked across the Red Sea bottom as the waters were held up by the power of God. The children of Israel made it across the sea just as the Egyptian army began to cross it. Moses again stretched out his hand, and the waters came crashing down, drowning all the Egyptians in pursuit.

Moses spent the next forty years in the wilderness with the children of Israel. There were many challenges during those forty years. Moses was able to institute a system of government. Some of its aspects are still used in democracies today. The practice of removing debts from credit reports after seven years comes from the Bible. You don't believe me? Let's look at Deuteronomy 15:1–2: "At the end of every seven years you shall grant a release of debts. And this is the form of the release: Every creditor who has lent anything to his neighbor shall release it; he shall not require it of his neighbor or his brother, because it is called the Lord's release."

Now let's think about the foolishness of God using Moses for a moment. Why would God use a man (Moses) with a speech impediment to lead a group of nearly one million people out of Egypt to the wilderness and become their leader? I will tell you. God uses the foolish things to confuse the wise. Why would God use an orphan (Moses) to write most of the Old Testament in the Bible? God did this because He uses the foolish things to confuse the wise. So stop making excuses for your past and allow God to use you.

Let's consider the anger that Moses struggled with before we move to the next chapter. The anger of Moses caused him to kill a man. An outburst of anger prevented Moses from entering the promised land. The land was promised to the Israelites by God. Moses was able to enter the ultimate promised land of heaven.

Anger leads people into actions they may regret. Anger is a time bomb waiting to explode if it is not dealt with properly. This book will highlight the flaws of each person mentioned but also show that God was still able to use them mightily. When you begin to doubt yourself, just remember Moses. God called upon a man who struggled with anger and a poor self-image, and this man became the mediator of the old covenant and the first author of scripture.

3

Rahab, the Harlot

We encounter Rahab in the second chapter of Joshua. Typically, the children of Israel would send out spies to scout out the land before they would move in to attack. The spies gathered information on the challenges they would face. Joshua had assumed command of the children of Israel from Moses. Joshua sent out two spies to view the land of Jericho. The two spies entered the land and came to the house of a harlot named Rahab. Someone in Jericho had told the king that men had come from Israel to search out the country. The king of Jericho sent word to Rahab that she needed to bring out the spies. Instead Rahab hid them. Rahab actually lied to the king by telling him that the men came and then left during the night. Rahab hid the men on her roof. Men from the city began to pursue them. Rahab went to the spies on the roof and told them she knew the Lord had given them the land of Jericho. Rahab told the spies how people in Jericho had heard about the Lord drying up the Red Sea for them to come out of Egypt. As the Lord was with Joseph, He was with the children of Israel. Word traveled about how the Lord God dried up the Red Sea for His children. Believe me, if you are truly serving the Lord, people will see signs of it. We don't need to be ashamed of our identity in Christ. I remember a prophet telling me that children of God do not have to make it known who they are because God will prove their identity. You can definitely see this with the children of Israel. People feared them based on what they heard.

Let's get back to Rahab. Rahab asked the spies to spare her and her family since she had shown the spies kindness. The spies told Rahab that they would grant her wish. Rahab then let the spies down by a rope through a window in her house. They escaped undetected. The spies told Rahab to bind a line of scarlet cord in the window before they left. They also told her to bring all her relatives into her house. Everyone who was in her house would be spared. The scarlet cord in the window had the same significance as the blood on the doorposts of the children of Israel in Egypt. Back in Exodus 12, we read of the tenth plague, which was the death of the firstborn children of the Egyptians. Moses instructed the children of Israel to take the blood of a lamb and place it on their doorposts. He also told everyone to stay in their houses until morning. The angel of death would not strike their homes with death if they obeyed these instructions. The scarlet cord on Rahab's window was a type and shadow of this. The scarlet cord on her window was a sign to the invaders to spare Rahab and her household. Both of these signs are symbolic of the blood of our sacrificial lamb, Jesus. There is no more need to put the blood of sacrificial lambs on our doorposts or tie scarlet cords on our windows. The blood that Jesus shed on the cross was the ultimate sacrifice.

Let's talk about harlotry for a moment. Can you imagine what the religious people of that time would think about God sparing a harlot? After all, isn't prostitution a sin? It's funny how we try to look at certain sins differently. I hate to break the news to you, but God looks at sin one way. In the eyes of God, sin is sin. Let's talk about homosexuality briefly before we move on. Some

Christians try to judge homosexuality like it is in some different category. Well, my friend, homosexuality is no different than fornication (sex while not married). Both are sinful in the eyes of God. Thank God that the blood of Jesus cleanses us. But the cowardly, unbelieving, abominable, murderers, sexually immoral, sorcerers, idolaters, and all liars shall have their part in the lake that burns with fire and brimstone, which is the second death, according to Revelation 21:8. God puts liars in the same category with murderers and sexually immoral persons. So your little white lie is not as insignificant as you may think. This should change all our perspectives on judging others. Maybe if we focus more on the person than the sin, we can reach more people for Christ. The answer is to walk in the love of God. The word of God tells us that "love suffers long and is kind; love does not envy; love docs not parade itself, is not puffed up; does not behave rudely, does not seek its own, is not provoked, thinks no evil; does not rejoice in iniquity, but rejoices in the truth," as we read in 1 Corinthians 13:4–6.

I would tell a homosexual person the same thing I would tell a fornicator: God loves you but not the sin or, for that matter, any sin.

Let me share one more scripture before I get back to Rahab.

> Then the scribes and Pharisees brought to Him a woman caught in adultery. And when they had set her in the midst, they said to Him, "Teacher, this woman was caught in adultery, in the very act. Now Moses, in the law, commanded us that such should be stoned. But what do You say?" This they said, testing Him, that they might have something of which to accuse Him. But Jesus stooped down and wrote on the ground with His finger, as though He did not hear. So when they continued asking Him, He raised Himself up and

said to them, "He who is without sin among you, let him throw a stone at her first." And again He stooped down and wrote on the ground. Then those who heard it, being convicted by their conscience, went out one by one, beginning with the oldest even to the last. And Jesus was left alone, and the woman standing in the midst. When Jesus had raised Himself up and saw no one but the woman, He said to her, "Woman, where are those accusers of yours? Has no one condemned you?" She said, "No one, Lord." And Jesus said to her, "Neither do I condemn you; go and sin no more."

(John 8:3–11)

This is one of my favorite scriptures—a great illustration of how God loves us unconditionally, even during our worst moments. Isn't it interesting that when Jesus told the group that the person without sin should cast the first stone, no one could do it? All of us have sin in our lives whether we want to admit it or not. Fortunately, God sees us through the eyes of Jesus and leaves a way for us to ask for forgiveness of our sins daily. The blood of Jesus was shed for our past, present, and future sins. Please don't misinterpret this generosity as a license to sin. If your heart is truly in the right place, you will try to find a way out of sin, not a way into sin. The way out of sin is Jesus Christ. We will discuss that a little later. I have enough trouble keeping myself out of sin; I don't have time to judge someone else.

A harlot is just as significant to God as Moses. That harlot has a mother, father, brother, and sister just like anyone else. A father doesn't love one of his children and not the others. Don't let anyone tell you that you are a failure and there is no hope for you. You are significant in the eyes of God, and He wants the best for you. God said you are the "apple of His eye." Rahab was accepted into the nation of Israel and married into the tribe of Judah. The tribe of Judah was in the lineage of Jesus Christ.

I can hear the Pharisees yelling "Heresy!" This doesn't make Jesus any less holy because He was conceived of the Holy Spirit and born of a virgin, as told in Matthew 1:20: "But while he thought about these things, behold, an angel of the Lord appeared to him in a dream, saying, 'Joseph, son of David, do not be afraid to take to you Mary your wife, for that which is conceived in her is of the Holy Spirit. Don't try to figure this out with your natural mind, it won't work.'" Rahab was also an ancestress of King David and other kings. That's a story you don't hear often: a harlot in the ancestry of kings. See it for yourself in the genealogy of Jesus Christ, the son of David and of Abraham. Abraham begot Isaac, Isaac begot Jacob, and Jacob begot Judah and his brothers. Judah begot Perez and Zerah by Tamar, Perez begot Hezron, and Hezron begot Ram. Ram begot Amminadab, Amminadab begot Nahshon, and Nahshon begot Salmon. Salmon begot Boaz by Rahab, Boaz begot Obed by Ruth, Obed begot Jesse, and Jesse begot David, the king. In Matthew 1:5, we learn that David, the king, begot Solomon by the lady who had been the wife of Uriah.

The fact that Rahab was previously a harlot didn't stop her from being used by God. It's time to stop making excuses for where you are, step out in faith, and let God use you. There were people who tried to discourage me from writing this book. People tend to think one's life has to be perfect to be used by God. I'm sorry, but there has only been one perfect person; and that person is Jesus Christ. I'm happy to know that God sees me through the blood of Jesus. Remember this the next time the enemy tries to bring condemnation.

4

Jephthah,
the Son of a Prostitute

Jephthah was the son of a harlot. He turned out to be a great warrior and leader. Jephthah didn't let the label "son of a harlot" determine his outcome. How have people labeled you? The word of God immediately refers to Jephthah as a mighty man of valor but says he was the son of a harlot. In Judges 11:1, we read, "Now Jephthah the Gileadite was a mighty man of valor, but he was the son of a harlot; and Gilead begot Jephthah." Did you notice that God referred to him as a mighty man of valor before mentioning that he was the son of a harlot? God likes to focus on the positive.

Romans 4:17 mentions that God calls those things that do not exist as though they did exist.

Let's discuss this for a moment. The scripture said that God calls those things that do not exist as though they did. This is why we read of Jephthah as a mighty man of valor even before his destiny was brought to fruition. God has done this throughout the scriptures. Abraham is a prime example. His original name was Abram before God changed his name to Abraham. *Abram* means *exalted father*. *Abraham* means *father of a multitude*. God changed his name because Abraham was to be the founding father of the

Jewish nation. God named him according to his future destiny and not by his present situation. God called him by his future, not by his past. If you are feeling worthless, I call you worthwhile. If you are feeling meaningless, I call you meaningful. Stop focusing on the negative and see what God says about you in His word.

Now let us go back to Jephthah. Jephthah's half-brothers forced him out of their household. The brothers told Jephthah that he would have no inheritance in their father's house because he was the son of another woman. This also reminds me of Joseph because he was also rejected by his brothers. The enemy loves to bring division. Situations such as these make a person experience rejection.

Rejection takes root in the heart and can open us to negative affects such as condemnation and unworthiness. We will get into condemnation in the last chapter of this book. Jephthah fled from his brothers and lived in the land of Tob. Sometimes we just have to get away from the negativity. Scripture notes that other worthless men banded together with Jephthah in Tob. Have you ever heard the saying, "Misery loves company"? These men all felt worthless, so they banded together and gave each other encouragement and comfort.

When the people of Ammon made war against Israel, the elders of Gilead went to get Jephthah from the land of Tob. The elders requested that Jephthah come to be their commander as they prepared to fight the Ammonites. Jephthah was confused about why the elders wanted him to be their commander. Jephthah reminded them that he was the same person whom they had rejected but consented to be their commander. Jephthah went with the elders of Gilead, and the people made him head and commander over them. Regardless of where you are currently, God knows how to find you and bring redemption. Notice that in the time of crisis, no one cared that Jephthah was the son of a harlot. I really believe that God gave us all these examples in the Bible as encouragement. No matter what you have in your past, God has plans for your future.

5

David,
an Adulterer and Murderer

David was a very interesting person. David is one of my favorites in the Bible. David is mentioned in the Bible at a time when the reigning king, Saul, was having a very difficult time. God lost patience with Saul and stripped the kingdom from him. Saul repeatedly disobeyed God, a story told in 1 Samuel 15:23. "For rebellion is as the sin of witchcraft, and stubbornness is as iniquity and idolatry. Because you have rejected the word of the Lord, He also has rejected you from being king." It is extremely important that we Christians obey God when He instructs us to do something. If we don't obey Him, God will find someone else to carry the torch. Let's get back to Saul. God was now ready to anoint a new king because of Saul's continued rebellion. The Lord sent the prophet Samuel to Jesse the Bethlehemite, David's father.

The Lord told Samuel that the new king was among Jesse's sons. Samuel was worried that Saul would hear about this and kill him. The Lord gave Samuel further instructions to quell the fear. Samuel went to Jesse as the Lord had instructed. Most of the things God calls a person to do will require courage. Samuel invited Jesse and his sons to go with him to sacrifice to the Lord.

The Lord spoke to Samuel as he was sacrificing. The Lord told Samuel not to look at the appearance or physical stature of the sons. We see again, God uses the foolish things. The Lord told Samuel something very interesting in 1 Samuel 16:7. The Lord told Samuel that the Lord does not see as man sees. The Lord told Samuel that man looks at the outward appearance, but the Lord looks at the heart. Seven of Jesse's sons passed before Samuel and were not chosen as the next king.

Jesse then allowed the eighth son, who was the youngest, to pass before Samuel. This son was David. The Lord immediately told Samuel to anoint David because he was the chosen one. God's mentality is definitely different from ours. How many of us would have the patience to wait on number eight?

It would take time before David eventually assumed the throne as king. That reminds me of the writing of this book. God gave me the vision of writing this book in 2005. Ten years later, I finally wrote the book. I will give that testimony at the end of this book.

Let's get back to Saul. The Spirit of the Lord departed from Saul, and a distressing spirit began to trouble him. Saul's servants sought someone who played the harp to come to Saul. The servants knew that a harpist would help relieve Saul of the distressing spirit. One of the servants said they knew that one of Jesse's sons was skilled in playing the harp. Guess which son it was? Nothing just happens. As only God would have it, David was the one chosen. This is another situation that seems foolish in our natural thinking. Why would God use the future king to help the former king? You can see all kinds of problems this could present. Surely Saul couldn't have been happy about losing the kingdom. That was like being fired and having to train your replacement. Saul sent a messenger to Jesse to send David to him. David came to Saul. Saul was very pleased with David, who became Saul's armor bearer. This was basically becoming Saul's right-hand man. God always believes in a preparation stage before you walk into your calling. Whenever the distressing spirit would come upon Saul, David would play the harp, and the spirit would depart. Saul's army went out to battle the Philistines, who were led by Goliath. Goliath was the Philistines' best fighter. He was also a giant. Goliath would often taunt Saul's army. Goliath challenged the army of Israel, saying that if they could send someone to defeat him and the Philistines, they would become servants of Israel. If Israel lost, they would become the servants of the Philistines.

The Israelites were afraid of Goliath and the Philistines at this time. Israel struggled continuously with its identity. God was in their corner, but Israel tended to forget this fact at times. Some of David's brothers were in this battle with Israel. There was an occasion where David brought food to his brothers on the battlefield. David heard Goliath challenging the army of Israel.

All the men of Israel, when they saw Goliath, feared him and fled. The men of Israel knew that Goliath came to defy Israel. The king of Israel even put a reward into play. He would reward the man who killed Goliath with great riches. The man who killed Goliath would also get the king's daughter in marriage.

David wanted to know who had defied the armies of the living God. Saul heard of David's words and sent for him. David told Saul he would fight with Goliath. Saul told David that he could not go up against Goliath because of his youth. Saul also noted that Goliath was more experienced than David.

Don't let people second-guess away what God has called you to do. God knows how to equip the young as well as the old. I bet a lot of successful business people heard, at some point, that they would fail. David told Saul of his previous victories. David mentioned his defeat of a lion after it took one of his lambs. David talked of defeating a bear as well. David began to speak faith. David mentioned that Goliath would be just like the bear and the lion. David didn't like Goliath defying the armies of the living God. David knew it was the Lord who had delivered him from the paws of the lion and bear, and he knew that the Lord would deliver him from the hand of the Philistine. Saul allowed David to go up against the giant after these declarations of faith. Declarations of faith carry great power. People automatically distinguish between faith and fear. You can always tell what is in the heart of a person by what comes from that person's mouth. Saul clothed David with his armor. David took off the armor because it was not tested. This is important. David took his own staff and chose five smooth stones and put them in a pouch. I believe God led David to take Saul's armor off for a specific reason: Saul could have taken credit for letting David wear his armor. God likes to put circumstances in place where only He can get credit.

Then it was time to face Goliath. David only had five stones, a staff, a bag, and a sling in his possession. There is one interesting point about Goliath that I forgot to mention. The Bible describes Goliath as six cubits and a span tall. Most biblical scholars equate that measurement to six feet and nine inches. Goliah would definitely be a giant to David, who was still a boy at the time. David moved toward Goliath. Real faith will cause you to move forward and act.

Goliath also moved toward David. Goliath saw David and immediately began to question his youth. We have the tendency to judge others by their outward appearance. Remember, God uses the foolish things.

Goliath threatened to give David's flesh to the birds of the air and the beasts of the field. David took note of Goliath's weapons. Goliath had a sword, a spear, and a javelin. David mentioned that he only came to Goliath with the name of the Lord. David knew that the Lord would deliver Goliath into his hands. David told Goliath he would strike him and take his head. David also told Goliath that all the earth would then know that there was a God in Israel. This was David still speaking more faith. A key remark by David was that the assembly would know that the Lord does not save with sword and spear, for the battle is the

Lord's, and He would give Goliath into his hands. Everything David said expressed faith. David didn't concentrate on how big, experienced, or intimidating Goliath was. Don't pay attention to how impossible the situation looks; nothing is impossible to God. Matthew 19:26 should close the deal. Jesus looked at them and said, "With man this is impossible, but with God all things are possible." David ran toward Goliath to meet him quickly, took one stone out of his bag, and placed it in a sling. That stone struck Goliath in the forehead, killing him instantly. David ran and stood over Goliath, drew his sword, and cut off Goliath's head. David was showing how to get a*head* in life. Get it? Okay, my dry humor is over.

Now let's examine this victory more closely. Here is David, a youth with the fire of God within him. We definitely see boldness in David. When you know who you are in Christ, there is a certain level of boldness that will come on you. You can be bold like the lion from the tribe of Judah, Jesus Christ. You will not see situations and circumstances as impossible when you operate boldly.

The army of Israel was full of experienced veterans. These were all grown men; David was still a youth. Tell me that wouldn't seem foolish to the world—sending a youth to fight the best and biggest warrior of the opposing army. David had experienced victory through God before with the killing of the bear and the lion. What circumstances and situations has God brought you through previously? Sometimes we have to remind ourselves of the point from which God has brought us. God wants you to remember what He has done previously. This should stir up your faith. If God has done it once, He will do it again. God is not a respecter of persons, but he is a respecter of faith. What do I mean by "God is not a respecter of persons"? I'm glad you asked that question. God does not show favoritism or partiality between believers. Faith is what He seeks. In Acts 10:34, Saint Peter affirmed this focus: "Then Peter opened his mouth and said:

In truth I perceive that God shows no partiality." Hebrews 11:6 confirms this idea: "But without faith, it is impossible to please Him, for he who comes to God must believe that He is, and that He is a rewarder of those who diligently seek Him."

David also faced Goliath without armor. This was unheard of during that time. The armor was obviously for protection. This was clearly another choice that was foolish. This parallels the New Testament scripture, Ephesians 6:11, that says we are to put on the whole armor of God: "Put on the whole armor of God that you may be able to stand against the wiles of the devil." David knew he had God's spiritual armor. David didn't have the traditional sword. David did possess the spiritual sword of his mouth, however.

As recorded in Hebrews 4:12, David spoke in faith as he might wield a sword: "For the word of God is living and powerful, and sharper than any two-edged sword, piercing even to the division of soul and spirit, and of joints and marrow, and is a discerner of the thoughts and intents of the heart."

As we discussed in the introduction to this book, God uses the foolish things to confuse the wise. He wants the nonbeliever to scratch his head in wonder and amazement. Remember, God said His ways are not our ways and His thoughts are not our thoughts. After David's victory through God, we see the men of Israel rise, shout, and pursue the Philistines. Stepping out in faith can propel others to do what God has called them to do. David took Goliath's head and brought it to Jerusalem to show everyone that God had given them the victory. Saul was pleased and appointed David over the men of war. This would probably be equivalent to being the secretary of defense in the American government. A young boy's promotion above men should catch everyone's attention. God uses the foolish things.

It is obvious that God had a hand in that situation. David was accepted by all the people. Can you see trouble around the corner? Do you think the enemy is actually going to stand back and allow this to happen without any attempt at distraction? Don't expect the enemy to give up trying to distract you from God's plan for your life. Notice the phrase *distract you*. No, he can't stop the plan of God unless you let him. The enemy is like a toothless lion: all growl but no bite. The enemy is a defeated foe. The only power he has is what we give him. This is why he seeks those whom he may devour. Be sober and vigilant because your adversary, the devil, walks about like a roaring lion, seeking those whom he may devour. Notice the simile: like a roaring lion. *Like* is the key word: He tries to imitate a roaring lion.

Let's get back to Saul. King Saul had a son named Jonathan. David and Jonathan became very close friends and made a covenant with one another. Remember, a covenant is a vow, pledge, or promise between two or more parties. This will come into play later.

As David was returning from the slaughter of Goliath to meet King Saul, the women came out of all the cities of Israel, singing and dancing, with tambourines, with joy and musical instruments. The women mocked King Saul by singing that David had slain more men in battle. Saul became very angry and displeased. Saul thought that now David could possibly have the kingdom. Apparently Saul forgot that he had already lost the kingdom. Saul eyed David from that day forward with envy. The next time a distressing spirit came upon Saul; David was there to play music as before. Saul had a spear in his hand as David played music. Saul threw the spear at David, but David escaped twice. Saul was afraid of David because the Lord was with him. Saul removed David from his position as his armor bearer and made him captain over a thousand men. David behaved wisely in all his ways, and the Lord was with him.

All of Israel and Judah loved David, and Saul was envious because of it. David married Michal, one of Saul's daughters. Saul saw that David experienced victory after victory. David became Saul's enemy

Saul made several failed attempts to kill David for no reason other than jealousy. God protected David each time. Whether we want to believe it or not, we all have an appointed time to leave this earth. Nothing can interfere with your appointed time. We don't have to fear death. Jesus has already defeated death.

And as it is appointed for men to die once, but after this the judgment, so Christ was offered once to bear the sins of many, as it is written in Hebrews 9:27–28. *Appointed*, in that scripture, means *to be reserved* in Greek. Okay, let's get back to David. On one occasion, Michal protected David by letting him down through a window to escape from Saul. Saul was furious with Michal for protecting David. There was another occasion when Jonathan (Saul's son) helped protect David. Jonathan got a sign from his father Saul that he was going to kill David. Jonathan was able to warn David so he could flee ahead of time. You see that God knows how to protect his children. God will even use someone in the enemy's camp to protect his children. We see two examples of God using Saul's son and daughter to help David. So much for the old saying that blood is thicker than water. Spiritual bonds are always closer than any other bond. God uses the foolish things to confuse the wise. I'm sure Saul was astonished that his own children were helping David.

David stayed in the wilderness and remained in the mountains to get away from Saul. Saul sought David every day, but God did not allow Saul to find him. Jonathan came into the wilderness to encourage David. Jonathan told David not to worry because Saul would not find him. Jonathan also reminded David that he would be king over Israel. We all need encouragement at times. You may not see how God will bring you to the place of your calling. Don't try to figure it out; just believe. If God told you to do something, He will bring it to pass no matter what it looks like currently. God is waiting for you to step out and do what He called you to do. Stop looking at it through your limited natural view. Open your spiritual eyes and see it through the avenues of faith.

There was an occasion where David and his men were in the wilderness. Saul found out that David was there in the wilderness and went looking for him with three hundred men. David and his men were hiding in a cave. Saul went into the cave to relieve himself. David secretly cut a piece of Saul's robe as he was in the cave. David was troubled that he did this to the king who was anointed by the Lord. Wow, that is something. Saul was trying to kill David constantly, and David felt bad about cutting Saul's robe. David was definitely a man who was in tune with God. David knew that Saul was still the king until God physically removed him. You definitely have to be patient while God brings the vision to pass. It would be a troubling thing to let your flesh get in the way of what God wants to do. This is why you have to seek God and His direction through prayer constantly. I will get into some specifics of moving into your God-given calling in the last chapter of the book. David also instructed his men not to harm Saul. David yelled to Saul as he was exiting the cave. David referred to Saul as his lord the king. David put his head down and bowed to the earth. David was truly a man who operated in humility.

Some people may see David's actions as weak, but I assure you that is not the case. As it is written in Titus 3:1–2, "Remind them to be subject to rulers and authorities, to obey, to be ready for every good work, to speak evil of no one, to be peaceable, gentle, showing all humility to all men." David told Saul that he shouldn't listen to men who told him that David wanted to do him harm. David told Saul that he could have taken his life in the cave at the urging of someone else. People will try to convince others to act outside the will of God. We have to be careful of listening to people instead of God. This is not to say we shouldn't listen to people at all. There is such a thing as godly counsel. Just be prayerful and let the peace of God in your heart be the deciding factor, as it is stated in Colossians 3:15 (AMP). This is why God gave us his Holy Spirit to lead and guide us. David told Saul that he would not lift his hand against him. Saul began to weep as he realized this was David's voice. Saul told David that he was more righteous than he because David rewarded him with good. Saul said he had only rewarded David with evil. Saul pronounced a blessing over David. Saul said that the Lord would reward David with good for what he had done. Saul also said he knew now that David would surely be king. Saul asked David to swear that he wouldn't cut off his descendants after him or destroy his name from his father's house. David swore to honor his wish. David left the presence of Saul. David continued hiding in the wilderness. Saul received word a second time where David was hiding. Saul took three thousand men and sought after David again. Saul went from three hundred to now three thousand men in pursuit of David. Saul could have brought three million men; it would not have made a difference. There is no number of men that can stop the plan of God. David saw Saul coming for him this time by sending out spies.

David went down into Saul's camp at night while they slept. One of David's men wanted to strike and kill Saul. David would not allow him to kill Saul. David said the Lord would not allow him to stretch out his hand against His anointed (Saul). So David and his men left without harming Saul.

David escaped from Saul to the land of the Philistines for a time. Saul found out that David was there and sought him no longer. David lived there one year and four months. The Philistines eventually rejected David. The Philistines did not want David and his men to go out to battle with them. Don't ever forget that everything happens for a reason.

Now the Philistines fought against Israel. The men of Israel fled and were slain by the Philistines. The Philistines now followed after Saul and his sons. The Philistines killed all Saul's sons. Saul was hit by an arrow and severely wounded. Saul asked his armor bearer to finish him off with his sword. The armor bearer initially wouldn't finish Saul off because he was afraid. Saul took the sword and fell on it, taking his own life. The armor bearer saw this and took his own life as well. A messenger came to David to inform him of the tragedy. David and his men immediately went into mourning. This was another display of his humility. Instead of celebrating Saul's demise, even though aware that he would be Saul's successor, David mourned.

David was initially made king of Judah for a season. David eventually became king of all of Israel. David was thirty years old when he became king over all of Israel. King David led Israel to many victories. David remembered the promise he made to Saul.

David had promised Saul that he wouldn't cut off his descendants after him or destroy his name from his father's house. David wanted to know if there was anyone from the house of Saul left to whom he could show kindness. There remained a son of Jonathan, Mephibosheth. Remember, Jonathan was Saul's son. King David brought Mephibosheth before him and told him he would show him kindness for Jonathan's sake. David told Mephibosheth that he would restore to him all the land of Saul. Showing kindness to Mephibosheth was a fulfillment of the promise David made to Saul. As the story is recounted in Acts 13:22, "And when He had removed him, He raised up for them David as king, to whom also He gave testimony and said, 'I have found David the son of Jesse, a man after My own heart, who will do all My will.'" I wanted to show you that scripture before we move on with David. Remember the phrase "a man after My own heart."

God knew that David would make mistakes even before David was even conceived. God knew that you would make mistakes as well. Stop letting the enemy tell you that God can't use you. Every person in the Bible made mistakes except Jesus. Those mistakes didn't stop all those people in the Bible from acting on God's will. They are no different from you except they stepped out on faith and let God do the rest. Now stop making excuses!

I want to share one last story about King David before we

move on to the next chapter. One evening David arose from his bed and walked out on the roof of his house. David saw a woman bathing, and the woman was very beautiful. David inquired about the woman and learned that she was the wife of Uriah. The woman's name was Bathsheba. David sent messengers and had Bathsheba brought to him. David slept with Bathsheba, and she became pregnant. Uriah was with the army during this event. David brought Uriah back from battle when he discovered Bathsheba was pregnant. I'm sure you can see trouble on the horizon. David told Uriah to go home to Bathsheba with the hope he would sleep with his wife. Uriah did not take the bait. Uriah slept at the door to the king's house with the other servants. David was surprised that Uriah didn't go to sleep with his wife. Uriah said he would do no such thing as long as the other men were in the battlefield. David asked Uriah to stay one more day. David ate and drank with Uriah until Uriah was drunk. David thought Uriah would go sleep with his wife since he was drunk. Uriah slept with the other servants again and didn't go to his house. This put David in a predicament. Now David arranged to put Uriah in the front of the battle line so he could be killed. David's plan worked, and Uriah was killed in battle. Bathsheba mourned the death of her husband Uriah. And when her mourning was over, David brought her to his house, and she became his wife and bore him a son. This action by David displeased the Lord greatly. God sent the prophet Nathan to David. Nathan told David a story about a rich man taking a poor man's lamb. David didn't know this story was about him initially. David became angry and told Nathan the rich man should die for doing this to the poor man. It's interesting how we want to hold others to a standard that we are not willing to maintain ourselves. We have to be very careful about judging others. Nathan began to prophesy to David, telling him that he was the rich man. Nathan reminded David how God anointed him king over Israel and delivered him out of the hand of Saul. Nathan reminded David how God gave him his master's house and wives. He also reminded David that God had given him the house of Israel and Judah. Nathan finally told David that if all those gifts were inadequate, God would have also given him much more. Let's look at the specific scripture.

Why have you despised the commandment of the

> Lord, to do evil in His sight? You have killed Uriah the Hittite with the sword; you have taken his wife to be your wife, and have killed him with the sword of the people of Ammon. Now therefore, the sword shall never depart from your house, because you have despised Me, and have taken the wife of Uriah the Hittite to be your wife. Thus says the Lord: Behold, I will raise up adversity against you from your own house; and I will take your wives before your eyes and give them to your neighbor, and he shall lie with your wives in the sight of this sun. For you did it secretly, but I will do this thing before all Israel, before the sun." So David said to Nathan, "I have sinned against the Lord." And Nathan said to David, "The Lord also has put away your sin; you shall not die. "However, because by this deed you have given great occasion to the enemies of the Lord to blaspheme, the child also who is born to you shall surely die." Then Nathan departed to his house.
>
> (2 Samuel 12:9–15)

Just because God called you to action does not mean you will not sin or make mistakes along the way. The real question is, "How will you respond?" Will you respond like David and take responsibility for your action? Or will you try to blame other people or things? This is one reason that God referred to David in the book of Acts as a "a man after my own heart." No matter the situation, David always took responsibility and quickly expressed repentance to God. This is what's missing in society today. People in general refuse to take responsibility for their actions. Remember, there are consequences for our sins. God will always forgive you if you ask. Just because you are forgiven doesn't mean there are no consequences for your actions. God spared David's life, but he suffered other consequences for his actions. God knew before the foundation of the world that David would make these mistakes, but He still chose to use David. God knew David's heart. God looks at the heart, not the outward appearance, as we read in 1 Samuel 16:7. It's just the opposite with people. People will look at your outward appearance or actions and not your heart. So we can say that David was an adulterer and a murderer, but God still chose to use him. I want to be very clear here; I'm not making excuses or condoning David's sins. I'm simply showing you that, although you have made mistakes, God can still use you to do great deeds. How can this be? Just remember this outcome is foolish in the eyes of the world but not foolish to God. God uses the foolish things! David was used by God to lead kingdoms and to write nearly half of the psalms— seventy-three of the 150 psalms. Read through the psalms and see David's heart. He was a man who loved God and constantly praised Him.

My own children may make mistakes, but that doesn't stop me from loving them and wanting the best for them. Well, my friend, God is no different. I hope that by now I've taken away most of your excuses for not stepping out on what God called you to do. I will work on the rest of your excuses through the next several chapters.

6

Gideon, the Fearful One

As is the pattern throughout the Bible, the Israelites again turned away from God after forty years of peace brought by Deborah's victory over Canaan. Deborah was a judge in the biblical sense. Following the conquest of Canaan by Joshua until the formation of the first kingdom of Israel, the Israelite tribes formed a confederation. No central government existed in this confederation, and in times of crisis, the people were led by judges. Deborah was one of these judges. The Israelites were subsequently oppressed by the neighboring Midianites and Amalekites due to turning away from God.

God chose Gideon, a young man from the tribe of Manasseh, to free the people of Israel and to condemn their worship of idols. We will see as we get into the story that Gideon was very unsure of himself and God's command.

Gideon displayed fear many times as God instructed him to do different things. Gideon's name was the opposite of the fear he displayed. Gideon means *destroyer* or *mighty warrior*. As it is written in Romans 4:17, "I have made you a father of many nations in the presence of Him whom he believed—God, who gives life to the dead and calls those things which do not exist as though they did." God called Gideon a mighty warrior before he stepped onto the battlefield. Gideon was fearful, but God called him "Mighty Warrior." This was God's practice throughout the Bible. He called Abraham *father of many nations* even while his wife Sarah was barren. God calls you a success even if you feel like a failure right now. No matter what people have told you, you are somebody in God's eyes.

> And an Angel of the Lord appeared to Gideon and said to him, "The Lord is with you, you mighty man of valor!" Gideon said to Him, "O my lord, if the Lord is with us, why then has all this happened to us? And where are all His miracles which our fathers told us about, saying, "Did not the Lord bring us up from Egypt?" But now the Lord has forsaken us and delivered us into the hands of the Midianites. Then the Lord turned to him and said, "Go in this might of yours, and you shall save Israel from the hand of the Midianites, Have I not sent you?"
>
> (Judges 6:12–14)

First of all, the Lord didn't forsake the Israelites as Gideon said. The actions of the nation of Israel led to the Midianites' oppression. The world in general blames God for things that are not His fault. We kick God out of our nation's schools and wonder why school violence is rampant. Prayer has been taken out of schools, and the Pledge of Allegiance has been removed because it makes reference to God. When prayer was in schools, we didn't have a flood of mass shootings in the schools.

Unfortunately, if this nation doesn't move back toward God, we will see many tragic events. I don't mean to be Mr. Doomsday, but God has shown us throughout the Bible what happens to a nation when it moves away from God. Wake up, America! Let's get back to Gideon. I thought it was very interesting that God chose Gideon to deliver the nation as he was complaining about the situation of the nation. Be careful what you complain about because you might be the one chosen to remedy the situation. Gideon responded to the call of God with an interesting comment in Judges 6:15. Gideon said, "O my Lord how can I save Israel? Indeed, my clan is the weakest in Manasseh, and I am the least in my father's house." Here is God continuing His practice of choosing the foolish things to confuse the wise.

Gideon's clan was the weakest in his city. Surely, Gideon must have thought, God would want to use the strongest clan. No, God wanted to use the clan that no one else would have chosen. Once again, God would get more glory out of using the weakest link than the strongest. A weak person would tend to lean on God more than someone who is strong. The strong person would naturally think that he could succeed through his own strength. In 2 Corinthians 12:9, God has said that He would be strong where we are weak—"And He said to me, 'My grace is sufficient for you, for My strength is made perfect in weakness. Therefore, most gladly I will rather boast in my infirmities, that the power of Christ may rest upon me.'"

Very unsure of both himself and God's command, Gideon requested proof of God's will by three miracles: first a sign from an angel, and then two signs involving a fleece, performed on consecutive nights, the exact opposite of each other. The Lord told Gideon to take his father's young bull, tear down the altar of Baal that his father had, and cut down the wooden image that was beside it. The Lord told Gideon to build an altar to the Lord and sacrifice a second bull. Gideon took ten men from among his servants and did as the Lord told him. But because Gideon feared his father's household and the men of the city too much to follow these commands by day, he did so by night. The next day, the men of the city saw the demolished altar of Baal and wooden image. They asked who had done this. They found out about Gideon and went to his father's house to kill him. Gideon's father, Joash, told the men that if Baal was a god, he would contend for himself. Then all the men gathered together and encamped in the valley, preparing for battle. The Spirit of the Lord came upon Gideon, and he blew the trumpet, and the Abiezrites gathered behind him. Gideon sent messengers throughout the land, and the men of those cities came up to meet them. Gideon asked God to show him a sign if he was going to save Israel. Gideon told God he would put a fleece of wool on the threshing floor. If there was dew on the fleece only, and the ground was dry, then Gideon would know that God would save Israel his hand. When Gideon rose early the next morning and squeezed the fleece, he wrung the dew out of the fleece, a bowl full of water. Gideon asked God not to be angry with him. Gideon requested the same sign, again this time with the fleece dry and the dew on the ground. And God did so that night. It was dry on the fleece only, but there was dew on the ground.

Then Gideon and all the people who were with him rose early and encamped beside a well so that the camp of the Midianites was on the north side of them. And the Lord told Gideon that the people with him were too many to have victory against the Midianites. God didn't want Israel to think their own hands saved them. Gideon told the people that anyone who was fearful should depart. And twenty-two thousand of the people returned, and then one thousand remained. The Lord thought one thousand was still too many people. The Lord wanted to test them. So Gideon brought the people down to the water. The Lord told Gideon that everyone who lapped from the water with his tongue, as a dog laps, should be set apart by himself; likewise, everyone who got down on his knees to drink. The number of those who lapped, putting their hands to their mouths, was three hundred men; but all the rest knelt to drink. The Lord told Gideon that he would save him by the three hundred men who lapped and deliver the Midianites into his hand.

God gave us a little insight into why he uses the foolish things to confuse the wise. God reduced Gideon's army from thirty-two thousand to three hundred men so Israel wouldn't claim glory for itself. God is a jealous God. Keep your ego out of the way and continuously give glory to God.

Gideon and the three hundred men were now ready for battle. The Lord woke Gideon in the middle of the night and told him to go down to the camp of the enemy. The Lord told Gideon to take his servant with him if he was afraid to go to the enemy's camp. The Lord knew Gideon struggled with fear, so he addressed it before Gideon could come up with an excuse. I found the way that God beat Gideon comical. The Lord told Gideon he would hear what the enemies were saying and that this would strengthen him.

Gideon and his servant went down to the outpost of the armed men who were in the camp. His enemies were lying in the valley, as numerous as locusts; their camels were without number, as the sand by the seashore. Gideon heard a man in the camp telling a dream to his companion. In the dream, the man said God had delivered their camp into the hands of Gideon. Gideon heard this and worshipped God. He returned to the camp of Israel and told the men that God had delivered the enemy into their hands. Then he divided the three hundred men into three companies, and he put a trumpet into every man's hand, with empty pitchers, and torches inside the pitchers. Gideon demonstrated what he wanted the men to do. Gideon told them that when he blew the trumpet, they should blow their trumpets all around the camp. Gideon also told them to shout, "The sword of the Lord and Gideon!" So Gideon and his three hundred men came to the outpost of the camp, just as they had posted the watch; and they blew the trumpets and broke the pitchers. The men then shouted,

"The sword of the Lord and Gideon!" And every man stood in his place all around the camp; and the whole army cried out and fled.

When the three hundred men blew the trumpets, the Lord set every man's sword against his companion throughout the whole camp, and the army fled. Absolutely brilliant! God led Gideon to create the illusion of a massive army with three hundred men. Gideon, in his own fearful assessment of his ability, would have never thought of this tactic. This outcome only happened through the wisdom of God. The Lord would go on to lead Gideon into several victories in battle. Then the men of Israel wanted Gideon to rule over them because he had delivered them from the Midianites. Gideon told them that he would not rule over them, but the Lord would rule over them. This was a great act of humility. Gideon then made a tragic mistake. Gideon asked the men of Israel for the golden earrings from the spoils of battle. That equates to about seventy pounds of gold today. Seventy pounds of gold is worth approximately 1.4 million dollars today. Gideon took the gold earrings and made an ephod of it. An ephod was an article of clothing and an object of worship in ancient Israeli culture, closely connected with priestly rituals. As the story is told in Judges 8:27, an interesting event happened after the ephod was set up. "Then Gideon made it into an ephod and set it up in his city, Ophrah. And all Israel played the harlot with it there. It became a snare to Gideon and to his house." This ephod eventually led to Israel again returning to the false god of Baal. We have to be careful not to let the values of the world distract us from the values of God. Remember God is a jealous God. I suppose Gideon forgot that God had previously made him tear down the wooden idol. The ephod played the same role as the wooden image did earlier. God knew Gideon would go down this path, but He still chose to use Gideon. You might think, "That doesn't make sense." Remember that God's thoughts are not our thoughts and His ways are not our ways. That's why He is God and we are not.

Let's focus on you for one moment. What's stopping you from moving toward what God called you to do? Is it fear, complacency, pride, money? Whatever your obstacle is, move it out of the way and let God be God in your life. Remember back in Exodus when God said, "I am?" *I am* _____. You fill in the blank and take away the excuses for not stepping out.

7

Samson, the Womanizer

The story of Samson took place during a time when God was punishing the Israelites by giving them into the hands of the Philistines.

> Again the children of Israel did evil in the sight of the Lord, and the Lord delivered them into the hand of the Philistines for forty years. Now there was a certain man from Zorah, of the family of the Danites, whose name was Manoah; and his wife was barren and had no children. And the Angel of the Lord appeared to the woman and told her she would conceive and bear a son. The angel then told the woman not to drink wine or eat anything unclean. She was told that a son would be conceived. The angel told her that no razor shall come upon her son's head, because the child would be a Nazirite to God from the womb; and he shall begin to deliver Israel out of the hand of the Philistines. (Judges 13:1–3)

A Nazirite is a person who vows, for a specific period, to abstain from certain practices, like partaking of grapes and any grape products, whether intoxicating or not, cutting his hair, or touching a corpse. It simply means to separate or dedicate oneself.

So Manoah bore a son and named him Samson. The child grew, and the Lord blessed him. And the Spirit of the Lord began to move upon him. Now Samson went down to Timnah and saw a woman of the daughters of the Philistines. Samson went up and told his father and mother that he had seen a woman in Timnah whom he wished to marry. His father and mother asked Samson if there was a woman among his own people who could be his wife. The Philistines were their enemies. Samson told his father he wanted the Philistine woman because she was right in his eyes. This appears to be a problem on the surface. His father and mother did not know that Samson's desire was inspired by the Lord—that He was seeking an occasion to move against the Philistines. At that time the Philistines had dominion over Israel. So Samson went down to Timnah with his father and mother and came to the vineyards of Timnah. To his surprise, a young lion came at him, roaring. And the Spirit of the Lord came mightily upon him, and he tore the lion apart as one would have torn apart a young goat, though he had nothing in his hand. Samson did not tell his father or his mother what he had done. Then he went down and talked with the woman; and she pleased Samson well. So his father went down to the woman. And Samson gave a feast there, for young men used to do so. When they saw Samson, they brought thirty companions to be with him. Samson told the men at the feast a riddle.

Samson told the men if they could solve the riddle, he would give them thirty linen garments and thirty changes of clothing. Samson told them they would have to give him the thirty linen garments and thirty changes of clothing if they could not solve the riddle. The men were eager to hear the riddle. Samson told them the riddle. For three days they could not explain the riddle.

On the seventh day, the men wanted Samson's wife to entice him to explain the riddle. The men threatened to burn her and her father's house if she wouldn't help them. Then Samson's wife appealed to him over the seven days of the feast. Samson told her the answer to the riddle on the seventh day because she pressed him so much. Then she explained the riddle to the sons of her people. So the men of the city tried to tell Samson the definition of the riddle. Samson knew then that the men got the information from his wife. This should have been a lesson to Samson.

Unfortunately, you will see later that he repeated his mistake. The next time would cost him dearly. Then the Spirit of the Lord came upon Samson mightily before they could tell him the riddle. Samson went down and killed thirty of their men, took their apparel, and gave the changes of clothing to those who had explained the riddle. Samson became very angry, and he went back to his father's house. Samson's wife was given to another man.

After a while Samson visited his wife with a young goat. Samson wanted to go into her room, but her father would not permit Samson to go in. Her father told Samson his daughter had been given to another man. Samson was not pleased about this. Samson went and caught three hundred foxes, took torches, turned the foxes tail to tail, and put a torch between each pair of tails.

When he had set the torches on fire, he let the foxes go into the standing grain of the Philistines and burned up the shocks and the standing grain, the vineyard, and olive groves. The Philistines found out that Samson had done this.

The Philistines then burned Samson's wife and her father. Samson told the Philistines he would take revenge on them. Samson attacked them with a great slaughter. Then he went down and lived in the cleft of the rock of Etam. The Philistines went up and encamped in Judah. The men of Judah inquired why the Philistines were encamped. The Philistines told Judah they were there to arrest Samson. Three thousand men of Judah went to Samson and reminded him that the Philistines ruled over them. They told Samson they had come to arrest him and turn him over to the Philistines. They tied Samson up and delivered him over to the Philistines. The Spirit of the Lord came mightily upon Samson as he was being turned over to the Philistines. The ropes holding Samson's hands came loose. Samson found a fresh jawbone of a donkey, reached out his hand and took it, and killed a thousand men with it.

Now Samson went to Gaza, saw a harlot there, and had relations with her. When the men of that city found out that Samson was there, they surrounded the place and lay in wait for him all night at the gate of the city. They plotted to kill Samson the following morning. Samson hid for a while, then arose at midnight and took hold of the doors of the gate of the city and the two gateposts. He pulled them up, bar and all, put them on his shoulders, and carried them to the top of the hill that faces Hebron.

Afterward Samson loved a woman in the Valley of Sorek. Her name was Delilah. And the lords of the Philistines came to Delilah and wanted her to entice Samson. They wanted Delilah to find out where his great strength lay and by what means they might overpower him. They wanted to bind and afflict Samson. They agreed to give Delilah eleven hundred pieces of silver. So Delilah asked Samson where his great strength lay and with what might he be bound to be afflicted. Samson told her that he could be bound with seven fresh bowstrings that were not yet dried. Then he would become weak like any other man.

So the lords of the Philistines brought her seven fresh bowstrings, not yet dried, and she bound Samson with them. Now men were lying in wait with her in the room. And she told Samson that the Philistines were upon him. But Samson broke the bowstrings as a strand of yarn breaks when it touches fire. So the secret of his strength was not known.

Samson tricked Delilah on three different occasions. Each time the Philistines tried, to no avail, to take advantage of Samson. Then Delilah told Samson that he didn't love her. Delilah told Samson he had mocked her three times and would not tell her where his great strength was. Do you see the pattern with Samson? And it came to pass, when she pestered him daily with her words and pressed him, so that his soul was impatient to the point of death, that he told her all his heart. Samson told her that no razor had ever come upon his head because he had been a Nazarite to God from his mother's womb. Samson told her that if he shaved, then his strength would leave, and he would become weak like any other man. When Delilah saw that he had told her all his heart, she told the lords of the Philistines to come up once more, because Samson told her all his heart.

So the lords of the Philistines came to her and put the money in her hand. Then she lulled Samson to sleep on her knees and called for a man to shave off the seven locks of Samson's head.

Then she began to torment him, and his strength left him. And she told Samson that the Philistines were upon him. So he awoke from his sleep and thought he would go out as before, at other times, and shake himself free. But he did not know that the Lord had departed from him. Then the Philistines took him, put out his eyes, and brought him to Gaza. They bound him with bronze fetters and put him in the prison. However, his hair grew again after it had been shaved. Now the lords of the Philistines gathered to offer a great sacrifice to Dagon, their god, and to rejoice.

The Philistines made a public statement that their god had delivered Samson, their enemy, into their hands. When the people saw Samson, they praised their god.

So it happened, when their hearts were merry, that they called for Samson to perform for them. They stationed him between the pillars. Then Samson asked the person who held him by the hand to feel the pillars that supported the temple. Samson told him he wanted to lean on the pillars. Now the temple was full of men and women. All the lords of the Philistines were there— about three thousand men and women were watching on the roof while Samson performed. Then Samson asked the Lord to remember him. He prayed for the Lord to strengthen him this one time. Samson told God that he wanted to take vengeance on the Philistines with one blow for his two eyes. Samson took hold of the two middle pillars that supported the temple and braced himself against them, one on his right and the other on his left. Samson shouted that he wanted to die with the Philistines. Samson pushed with all his might, and the temple fell on the lords and all the people in the building. He killed more people at that one time than ever previously.

Let's consider how foolish it seemed for God to use Samson. Samson came from the tribe of Dan, which was the weakest of the twelve tribes of Israel. Do you see the pattern? Let's think about this for a moment. Only God would have chosen that the strongest man who ever lived would come from the weakest tribe of Israel. We probably would have chosen someone from the strongest tribe if left to our human thinking. Not so with God; He uses the foolish things to confuse the wise! God even used Samson again after his mistake. Don't ever think God will give up on you. If you can repent, turn from your wicked ways, and seek the Lord, He will be there to answer you and restore you. Look at the nation of Israel. There were countless times when Israel turned against God, but He was always there to restore them once they truly repented. It's time to come out of that condemnation and shame. God is waiting for you.

Now let's talk about Samson's weaknesses. Samson, a mighty man of God, was awesome when he focused on his God-given assignments. Samson let the beauty of a woman distract him as King David, King Solomon, and countless others have done. We all have distractions from our continuous search for God's will. The enemy knows what will distract each of us. The enemy will bring that very distraction to divert us from God's plan. What is distracting you? I'm sure that you know what the distraction is. It's just a matter of your willingness to sacrifice your plan for God's plan. If there is a person, place, or thing that is continually causing you to fall, get it out of your life. As it is written in Hebrews 12:1, "Therefore, we also, since we are surrounded by so great a cloud of witnesses, let us lay aside every weight, and the sin which so easily ensnares us, and let us run with endurance the race that is set before us." God ordained for Samson to marry his Philistine wife for a specific purpose. Look at Judges 14:4. It was against God's law for the children of Israel to marry an uncircumcised person. In this instance, God wanted Samson to do it for a purpose. The purpose was for Samson to get angry and destroy the Philistines. God also did this with the prophet Hosea.

God wanted Hosea to love a harlot to experience what God had experienced when Israel looked to false gods. See Hosea 3:1–3. Delilah, on the other hand, was a different story. There is never any mention of Delilah being a part of God's plan for Samson. Delilah was a harlot. Samson slept with her and fell in love. The lords of the Philistines saw their opportunity to get to Samson.

On several different occasions, Samson saw that Delilah was trying to set him up. You would think that would have kept Samson from revealing the source of his strength to Delilah. Our emotions can blind us if we let them, rather than God, lead us. In this case, yielding to his emotions blinded Samson physically as well as spiritually. We believers have to be careful not to connect with nonbelievers in marriage or other romantic relationships. In 2 Corinthians 6:14 (AMP), we are advised, "Do not be unequally yoked with unbelievers [do not make mismatched alliances with them or come under a different yoke with them, inconsistent with your faith]." Samson's connection to Delilah is an example of such an alliance. King Solomon's love life also offers example of such wrongful alliances. King Solomon loved many foreign women. The Lord had told the nation of Israel not to intermarry with persons of certain nations. God warned them that these women would turn their hearts after their gods. This is exactly what happened to Solomon. These women turned Solomon's heart toward their gods. God doesn't tell us not to be unequally yoked because He is a mean God. God gives these instructions for our protection. He loves us and wants the best for us. God has to be first in our lives—above everything and everyone. This includes spouses. God is a jealous God and will not accept second place in our lives. You may have done some terrible things, but God has not given up on you. Now get up out of that misery and do what God has called you to do. We read this advice in Isaiah 60:1 (AMP): "Arise [from the depression and prostration in which circumstances have kept you—rise to a new life]! Shine (be radiant with the glory of the Lord), for your light has come, and the glory of the Lord has risen upon you!"

8

Paul, the Persecutor of the Early Church

What a story was the apostle Paul's! Paul was a persecutor of the early church but became an apostle called to preach the good news to the gentiles. *Gentile* was a term used in the Bible to refer to non-Israelites. Paul persecuted the early followers of Jesus Christ and tried to destroy the Christian church. Isn't the choice of such a man foolish in the eyes of the world? God was using a man who had tried to destroy the church to build the church and spread the good news.

Paul turned out to be one of the most influential early Christian missionaries and leaders of the church. God's ways are definitely not our ways, and His thoughts not our thoughts. Paul was known as Saul early in the book of Acts.

Saul is mentioned in the Bible immediately after the stoning death of Stephen. Stephen had been falsely accused of blasphemy, just as Jesus was. Stephen was stoned to death as he was preaching to the high priest about the killing of the prophets. Saul consented to the death of Stephen. As a matter of fact, Saul was present when Stephen was stoned. Around the time of Stephen's death, Saul was known for dragging men and women out of their homes and committing them to prison for their faith in Jesus. The conversion of Saul involved the direct intervention of Jesus Christ.

Saul was on his way back from the high priest with letters addressed to the synagogues in Damascus. These letters were for the arrest of any followers of Jesus. Saul thought he was going to arrest Christians, but he was arrested in the spirit by the Lord Jesus himself. Suddenly a bright light from heaven was all around Saul, and he fell to the ground. Jesus asked Saul why he was persecuting Him. Jesus said specifically that Saul was persecuting Him even though Jesus was in heaven at the time.

This brings to light an interesting point. We need to be careful how we treat one other. There is a parable told by Jesus in Matthew 25:31–40 that gives us a picture of this need.

> When the Son of Man comes in His glory, and all the holy angels with Him, then He will sit on the throne of His glory. All the nations will be gathered before Him, and He will separate them one from another, as a shepherd divides his sheep from the goats. And He will set the sheep on His right hand, but the goats on the left. Then the King will say to those on His right hand, "Come, you blessed of My Father, inherit the kingdom prepared for you from the foundation of the world: for I was hungry and you gave Me food; I was thirsty and you gave Me drink; I was a stranger and you took Me in; I was naked and you clothed Me; I was sick and you visited Me; I was in prison and you came to Me." Then the righteous will answer Him, saying, "Lord, when did we see You hungry and feed You, or thirsty and give You drink? When did we see You a stranger and take You in, or naked and clothe You? Or when did we see You sick, or in prison,

and come to You?" And the King will answer and
say to them, "Assuredly, I say to you, inasmuch as
you did it to one of the least of these My brethren,
you did it to Me."

(Matthew 25:31–40)

That scripture should make us very conscious of how we treat
others. I heard a friend of mine make an interesting remark about
driving. He said, "Would you have road rage if Jesus was sitting
next to you in a car?" Good point! Well, if you are a professing
believer, the Holy Spirit is present with you always. (Sorry, I don't
have time in this book for complete instruction on the Holy Spirit.)

Let's get back to Saul. Saul was blinded on this road to
Damascus and remained blind for three days. The number
three signifies completion or perfection and unity. I'm sure the
significance of the number is the reason that the Lord chose to
blind Saul for three days.

Jonah spent three days and three nights in the belly of the fish.
Jesus said, "Destroy this temple, and in three days I will raise it
up." This is just some food for thought.

Jesus specified that Saul was a chosen vessel of His to bear His
name before the Gentiles, kings, and the children of Israel. Saul
immediately went forth to preach after his sight was restored, and
he spent some time with the disciples at Damascus. Of course Saul
drew a lot of attention and amazement since he had previously
been a persecutor of the Christians.

The word of God mentions that Saul confused the Jews in
Damascus. I'm sure it was astonishing to see a man who had
previously condemned Jesus now preaching Jesus. Here we go
again: "God uses the foolish things to confuse the wise." Saul,
now persecuted himself, spoke boldly about Jesus.

The Bible shows that Saul was also called Paul in Acts 13:9. We
will refer to Saul as Paul from this point on. Let's talk a little about
Paul's past. Don't think for a minute that people will not bring

up your past as you move forward with the plan of God for your life. It happened to Paul, so be assured that it will happen to you.

We see this happening in Acts 9:13 as the Lord told Ananias to put his hands on Paul to restore his sight. Ananias told the Lord that he heard about how much harm Paul had done the saints in Jerusalem. This is when the Lord told Ananias that He had chosen Paul. You see, saints, don't let people stop you from what the Lord is calling you to do. It doesn't matter what they think of you. It only matters what the Lord thinks of you. I can tell you right now that you matter to God. You are somebody to God. Stop making excuses and get started on what God told you to do!

One thing I can say about Paul—he never denied his past even though he was a changed man. Several times Paul mentioned his past. Paul mentioned, in Galatians 1:13, his former conduct in persecuting the church of God. In 1 Timothy 1:13–16, he admitted that he was formerly a blasphemer, a persecutor, and a violently arrogant man. He said that mercy was obtained because of the grace of God. This mercy shows long-suffering as a pattern to future believers. There is one additional instance of Paul mentioning his past in 1 Corinthians 15:9–10. Paul referred to himself as the least of the apostles because he had once persecuted the church. Paul said that the grace of God had made him what he had become. So if people want to know how you moved from your past into what God called you to do, the grace of God, my friend, is the answer. Now we see why Paul talked so much about the grace of God in the New Testament.

Paul continued preaching the good news, healing people, and making disciples through the book of Acts. Paul was a great vessel for the Lord's power. Paul never took credit for anything. He knew all these deeds were done by the Lord. Remember that as you move into what God calls you to do. Never take credit for anything in the process. Give God the glory for everything. Paul also continued to be persecuted, jailed, beaten, and even stoned. None of these dangers stopped Paul. This story of Paul should motivate you to move forward in what God has called you to do.

Noah and Abraham, the Drunkard and the Doubter

Noah

The story of Noah was an interesting culmination of events. God was fed up with man at this moment in time. The wickedness and sin of man was great in the earth. Noah was not the foolish thing God used in this case. The foolish thing was the ark itself.

First of all, some biblical scholars believe it took around ninety-eight years to build the ark. Ninety-eight years? Can you imagine the number of skeptics and scoffers probably teasing Noah during this time? It is not easy to walk by faith when you don't see the end result. It's easy to believe when you can see. The disciple Thomas is a great example of this. Thomas walked with Jesus in the flesh but still struggled to believe at times. Jesus appeared to the disciples after His resurrection. Thomas made a statement, prior to seeing Jesus, that he would only believe if he saw the marks on the hands of Jesus, put his finger where the nails had been, and put his hands into His side. Jesus appeared before the disciples after His resurrection and told Thomas to touch Him and see. He told Thomas to touch His hands and to put his hand into His side. Thomas believed only after doing so. Jesus said that people who believe without seeing first are blessed.

The Bible doesn't tell exactly where Noah built the ark. According to some biblical scholars, it was built in a desert. Wow, isn't it foolish to build an ark in the middle of a desert? Just think, if the flood had never come, the ark would not have moved. I want you to imagine how big the ark was. The playing field of a professional football team in a domed stadium has a length of 360 feet. The overall length of this structure from the exterior is 745 feet.

Noah's ark was approximately 515 feet in length. So the next time you are at a football game, consider that the ark was probably about 155 feet longer than most professional football fields. The ark also was about seventy-five feet high and had three different levels. What a sight that must have been back in the days of Noah.

In Luke 17:26–27, Jesus confirmed that there had been people who didn't believe God would destroy the earth by flooding. Jesus mentioned that, as in the days of Noah, it would be the same on the earth upon His return. Specifically, Jesus mentioned that people were marrying, eating, and drinking up until the day Noah entered the ark. Then the flood came and destroyed them all.

In other words, people were ignoring the warnings of the coming flood. That sounds a lot like the present. The signs of the Lord's return are all around us, but people are ignoring them. Global warming, greenhouse gases, El Niño, and other indicators are the excuses given for the strange weather patterns.

In 2 Timothy 3:1–5 is a summary of the attitudes of people in general these days: "But know this, that in the last days perilous times will come: For men will be lovers of themselves, lovers of money, boasters, proud, blasphemers, disobedient to parents, unthankful, unholy, unloving, unforgiving, slanderers, without self-control, brutal, despisers of good, traitors, headstrong, haughty, lovers of pleasure rather than lovers of God, having a form of godliness but denying its power." Unfortunately, they will ignore the current signs as in the days of Noah.

God gave Noah specific instructions on the construction of the ark. There was a specific type of wood, specific dimensions, and specific instructions about the animals.

God is a specific God, and He knows how to give specific instructions. God has given me specific instructions in the writing of this book. God showed me the specific people in the Bible to write about, the specific audience (believers) to address, and He also showed me the specific title for the book. People tried to tell me the title of this book was wrong, but God said otherwise. I chose to obey God rather than man. What do you choose? Do you choose God or man?

Knowing you heard from God will keep you grounded when circumstances challenge your faith. The challenges will be specific challenges to the specific deeds(s) that God told you to do. Stop trying to figure it all out, step out, and begin the journey. You may not have every significant detail at the moment, but God will reveal those things to you at the right moment. You have enough faith to step out, but excuses are hindering you. It's time to move the excuses out of the way and let God be God.

Let's consider Noah before we move on to Abraham. Noah was a drunkard. Yes, the man whom God chose to replenish the earth after the flood was a drunkard. "And Noah began to be a farmer, and he planted a vineyard. Then he drank of the wine and was drunk, and became uncovered in his tent," according to Genesis 9:20–21.

Once again, this shows the human side of a man whom God used. No, he wasn't perfect, but God still used him. The Bible tells us not to be drunk with wine, so why would God use Noah? As I have said over and over again in this book, God is not looking for the perfect person. The world may try to convince you that you, as a Christian, have to be perfect. Don't buy into the lie. God knows we have made mistakes. God also knows that we will make more mistakes in the future. I'm chipping away at any excuse you may have regarding stepping out into what God called you to do. God uses the foolish things to confuse the wise!

Abraham

Abraham was another person whose name was changed by God. His original name was Abram. Abram means *exalted father.* We will discuss later why God changed his name to *Abraham.* God starts off with Abram by getting him out of his comfort zone. God instructs Abram to get out of his country, away from his family, out of his father's house, and to a land that God was going to show him. God didn't initially tell Abram where he was going when he departed. Abram departed as the Lord instructed. Abram was seventy-five years old at the time.

Imagine that you are seventy-five years old. Then imagine the Lord telling you to pack up everything you have, leave your relatives, and go to a place that God doesn't show you initially. Now that took some faith. As Abram departed, God then showed him the land of Canaan. This reminds me of when Peter stepped out on the water to meet Jesus. Peter stepped out of the boat without thinking and was actually walking on the water. The point is to step out and let God go to work on your behalf.

It was not until Abram departed that God showed him where he was going. That is some faith. How difficult would it be for you to leave your current home and go to a place that God would later show you? Abram did it without question even before he knew specifically where he was going. I would consider that foolish. Let's think about this a little more. A person packs up everything he has, moves away from his family, and departs without knowing exactly where he is going. This makes absolutely no sense. Well, apparently God doesn't think the way we think.

Abram finally settled in Canaan. There God told him to lift his eyes and look north, south, east, and west. God told him that all the land he saw would become the inheritance of his descendants. He also told Abram that his descendants would be as the dust of the earth—so many that one could not count them. However, at that time, Abram had no sons. How would his lineage continue without a son? God told Abram he would give him a son. God showed Abram the stars in the sky. God told Abram that his descendants would be as the stars, beyond a specific number. God did two more things to cement this in Abram's brain. God wanted to give Abram a visual. God also made a blood covenant with Abram. I will briefly touch on the process involved in blood covenants. A blood covenant sealed a binding contract between two men. Blood covenants would typically involve the following steps.

1. Two people would exchange coats or robes. To people of that time, the coat or robe represented the person himself; when he offered the other person his robe, he was offering himself, even his life.

2. They would then take off their belts, and each would offer the other his belt. The belt, also called the girdle, was used to hold a sword, knife, or other weapon. Offering the other a belt, a man offered that person protection. The other person's battles would become his battles.

3. Then an animal was killed and cut down the middle, and the two halves were laid opposite each other. The two parties to the covenant passed between the two halves of the animal and said, "May God do so to me, and more, if I break this covenant." A blood covenant could not be broken except by death.

4. Then the two parties raised their right arms, cut their palms, and clasped hands to mingle their blood. In this ritual, each said to the other person, "We are becoming one with each other." To mingle the blood was to connect the very lives of both people.

5. Then they exchanged names. Each took part of the other's name and incorporated it into his own.

6. Then they created a scar or some identifying mark. The scar was the outward and visible evidence of the covenant. The wedding band is the symbol used in marriage covenants.

7. Then the two parties stated the terms of the covenant. Both parties to the covenant stood before a witness and listed all their assets and liabilities. By this declaration they stated, "Everything I have is yours, and everything you have is mine."

Genesis 15–17 details the blood covenant that God established with Abram. Abram was ninety-nine years old when God established this covenant with him. The second thing God did to cement this covenant in Abram's brain was changing Abram's name to Abraham. From then on, when people said the name *Abraham*, they were saying, "Father of many nations." God also changed the name of Abraham's wife from Sarai to Sarah. The meaning of *Sarah* is "mother of nations." The covenant specifically said that Abraham would be a father of many nations, giving his descendants the land God promised. Abraham would, of course, have to endure some challenges on the journey to the fulfillment of the covenant.

First of all, his wife Sarah did not exercise faith in the promise of God. Abraham and Sarah both thought they were too old to produce children. Remember that God uses the foolish things to confuse the wise. Sarah even talked Abraham into sleeping with his Egyptian maidservant because she didn't think she could conceive. The Egyptian maidservant, Hagar, became pregnant and bore Abraham a son. The son was named Ishmael. Sarah became jealous, so Hagar and Ishmael were sent away into the wilderness.

God blessed Ishmael and told him he would multiply him

exceedingly. God promised to make Ishmael a great nation. We see the fulfillment of this promise to Ishmael in the oil wealth of the Arab nations. This one act of disobedience by Sarah, her use of Hagar as a surrogate, has caused conflict between the Arabs and Israelites that continues to this day. This is a major reason why there is so much fighting and turmoil in the Middle East now. Israel is continuously fighting with its Arab neighbors. It is amazing how one act can have such an impact on so many people. There is one final matter we need to talk about in reference to Abraham. God wanted to see if Abraham would trust him. God told Abraham to sacrifice Isaac—the one son Abraham would need to fulfill the covenant. Abraham took Isaac to a certain place and told his servants that he and the lad would come back to them. Whether he realized it or not, Abraham was speaking faith. Abraham knew he was going to sacrifice his son but told the servants that they both would return. Isaac also asked Abraham where God was going to get the lamb for the sacrifice. Abraham told Isaac that God would provide for Himself the lamb for a burnt offering. Abraham was once again speaking faith. Abraham put Isaac on the altar for sacrifice, and the Angel of the Lord called out to him as he lifted the knife to slay Isaac. The Angel of the Lord told Abraham not to lay a hand on Isaac. Abraham looked up and then saw a ram waiting in the bush.

Abraham then sacrificed the ram. Abraham named the place of the sacrifice Jehovah-Jireh, which means *the Lord will provide*. This is an important aspect of God to remember: Jehovah-Jireh— *the Lord will provide*. You need to understand that if God tells you or calls you to do something, He will definitely provide the resources. So stop making excuses and start stepping out and doing what God told you to do. God was still able to use Abraham even though he displayed unbelief and doubt at times. Sarah and Abraham didn't allow God's plan to develop. Don't think that you can mess up the plan of God. God has many different ways He can bring His plan to pass. So don't think your divorce, your child out of wedlock, or anything else will stop God from using you. Abraham still became "Father of Many Nations." What vision waits for you to fulfill it?

10

The Faith Blockers: Guilt, Shame, and Condemnation

I refer to guilt, shame, and condemnation as faith blockers. You will clearly see how these three are somewhat similar but have important differences. All three often work together to keep you from reaching your full potential for God. This is probably the most important chapter in this book, so pay close attention.

Guilt

Guilt is a very interesting word. Guilt is defined as a bad feeling caused by knowing or thinking that you have done something bad or wrong. The original Hebrew meaning of *guilt* is *fault, sin,* or *trespass*. The original Greek meaning is *a penalty, to be under obligation,* or *to be bound.* So you can readily see that guilt is a very good tool for the enemy to use against you. The initial guilty feeling should push us to ask for forgiveness and repent of the sin. If it lingers after you have asked for forgiveness, there is a slight problem. The enemy wants you to remain in guilt even after asking God for forgiveness. Guilt will keep you in a sin consciousness as well as keep you bound by the enemy if you let it linger. Just think of it as dragging a chain attached to your leg with heavy weights on it. Guilt will keep you from operating in faith. Many people spend their entire lives running from the past. We all have regrets and past actions that we wish we could change. These thoughts from guilt run rampant and eventually lead to shame if not dealt with properly. Your past will control your future if you fail to deal with it. Your past will keep you punishing yourself, which will lead to continued negative thinking. Just think about the guilt of Cain in Genesis 4. Cain killed his brother Abel, and the guilt from the offense disconnected him from God. The guilt of Judas from his betrayal of Jesus caused Judas to commit suicide.

Cain became a vagabond who wandered from place to place without a fixed home. The guilt troubled him so that he could not settle in one place for very long. A person who wanders without a purpose is just where the enemy wants him. You have a past, but that doesn't mean you have to be enslaved by it. God knew you before you were in your mother's womb. God knew every turn your life would take.

There is no circumstance or situation that can stop God's plan for your life. God has proven this throughout the Bible. God has used people from various backgrounds. God has crossed all boundaries—generational, racial, ethnic, gender, and religious. Stop putting God in a box. Nothing is impossible to God. Consider Paul's attitude in Philippians 3:13–14—"Brethren, I do not count myself to have apprehended; but one thing I do, forgetting those things which are behind and reaching forward to those things which are ahead, I press toward the goal for the prize of the upward call of God in Christ Jesus."

Paul knew his past would be a hindrance if he didn't let it go. The fact that I can't change the past helps me move beyond it. If you can't change the past, why are you spending so much time and energy dwelling on it? This is the main reason God moved from the law to grace. James 2:10 sums this up: "For whoever shall keep the whole law, and yet stumble in one point, he is guilty of all."

The law keeps you in a sin consciousness. Grace keeps you focused on the righteousness of God. We need to have a righteousness consciousness, not a sin consciousness. Just know that Jesus died on the cross and took care of guilt. Jesus took on guilt so you can be free from it. We now have an advocate, Jesus, with the Father, God, who pleads our case through His shed blood. This just simply means you are pronounced righteous and not guilty. Now tell the enemy that you are righteous and that he can have his guilt back because it's not yours anymore. This point is stated in Romans 5:18: "Therefore, as through one man's offense judgment came to all men, resulting in condemnation, even so through one Man's righteous act the free gift came to all men, resulting in justification of life."

Shame

Shame is defined as guilt, regret, or sadness felt because of one's awareness of wrongdoing. Did you see how close that definition was to guilt, a bad feeling caused by *knowing or thinking* that one has done something bad or wrong? Shame moves a person from a bad feeling to regret and sadness. The original Hebrew meaning of *shame* is *confusion*. The original Greek meaning of *shame* is *to confound or confuse*. Here is how guilt and shame work together. First we feel guilty for doing something wrong or bad. This is actually how we should feel initially. Initial guilt should drive us to ask God for forgiveness through prayer and then repent of the action. We allow shame to come in when we let guilt linger without dealing with it. Shame then drives a person to try to hide the action instead of dealing with it.

Shame first showed up in the garden of Eden. Shame will cause one to flee from the presence of God. We see this with Adam and Eve in Eden. I heard someone say a long time ago that we should run to God when shame hits us rather than flee Him. Sometimes we forget that God's love for us is unconditional. The enemy loves to play with our feelings and emotions. There are three aspects of shame that we need to consider.

The first aspect of shame is confusion. Shame will bring confusion. "Let them be confounded because of their shame," as the psalmist wrote in Psalm 40:15. To be confounded is to be confused. The reason shame brings confusion is because there are so many crazy thoughts that go through the mind. You are constantly thinking of things you could have done differently in the past. Read the book of Job if you want to see confusion at full power. Job's confusion caused him to ramble and make untrue comments about God. Job rambled on for thirty-seven chapters. God heard enough of Job's rambling and began correcting him in Job 38. Confusion can lead to so many other things. Ambivalence, alternating between the positive and the negative, is another hazard of confusion.

This presents a problem because God says, in the book of James, that a double-minded man is unstable in all his ways and unable to receive anything from the Lord. Now you can see how the enemy uses this to his advantage. If the enemy can keep a person in a double-minded state, that person, who is not operating in faith, will not receive anything from the Lord.

Shame is visible. The next aspect of shame is visibility. "We can't escape the constant humiliation; shame is written across our faces," as the psalmist wrote in Psalm 44:15 (NLT). A person operating in shame looks ashamed. I can look at a person's face and tell when that person feels ashamed. A person who is ashamed can't maintain eye contact and constantly looks for a way to get away. Shyness, in some cases, has shame attached to it.

Unrepentant sin and disobedience bring shame. The next aspects of shame are unrepentant sin and disobedience.

> For shame has devoured the labor of our fathers
> from our youth, their flocks and their herds, their
> sons and their daughters. We lie down in our
> shame, and our reproach covers us. For we have
> sinned against the Lord our God, We and our

fathers, from our youth even to this day, and have
not obeyed the voice of the Lord our God.
(Jeremiah 3:24–25)

The best way to explain this one is with another scripture, 1 John 1:9: "If we confess our sins, He is faithful and just to forgive us our sins and to cleanse us from all unrighteousness." Shame will begin to develop within a family when generational sins continue within the family and no one repents and confesses that sin. God is waiting for someone in the family to step up and rid the family of that generational sin. God has given us some instructions on how to deal with shame in Romans 9:33: "Behold, I lay in Zion a stumbling stone and a rock of offense, and whoever believes on Him will not be put to shame." In Romans 10:10–11, we read, "For with the heart one believes unto righteousness, and with the mouth confession is made unto salvation. For the scripture says, 'Whoever believes on Him will not be put to shame.'" When you accept Jesus as your Lord and Savior, He takes care of the shame. Stop letting the enemy put shame in your mind. Your mind needs to be renewed with the word of God. I will talk at the very end of this chapter about dealing with those negative thoughts of shame.

> Therefore, since we have this ministry, as we have received mercy, we do not lose heart. But we have renounced the hidden things of shame, not walking in craftiness nor handling the word of God deceitfully, but by manifestation of the truth commending ourselves to every man's conscience in the sight of God. (2 Corinthians 4:1–2).

God wants us to renounce shame. Renunciation is declaring, especially in a formal or official way, that we will no longer accept (something), that we formally give up something, that we say in a formal or definite way that we refuse to follow, obey, or support (someone or something) any longer. Rise and tell the enemy that you renounce shame and will no longer allow it to control your life. Do it now! Open your mouth and renounce it. There will be a prayer for you at the end of this book.

Condemnation

Condemnation is defined as a statement or expression of very strong and definite criticism or disapproval. Both the Hebrew and Greek meanings of *condemnation* are *adverse sentence, judgment,* and *accusation.* A key word among those definitions is *accusation.* I mentioned earlier that I would refer to the devil or Satan as *the enemy.* Well, accusation is the enemy's top weapon. Saint John refers to the enemy as the accuser of the brethren.

> Then I heard a voice saying in heaven, 'Now salvation, and strength, and the kingdom of our God, and the power of His Christ have come, for the accuser of our brethren, who accused them before our God day and night, has been cast down. (Revelation 12:10)

I will use several scriptures to help you see how the enemy uses condemnation against you. We were all condemned due to the actions of Adam and Eve in the garden. Jesus came down from heaven and died on the cross to fix what Adam and Eve messed up. Thank God that, after the death of Jesus on the cross, we are now justified or acquitted.

> And the gift is not like that which came through the one who sinned. For the judgment which came from one offense resulted in condemnation, but the free gift which came from many offenses resulted in justification. (Romans 5:16)

I mentioned previously that we were declared not guilty by the blood of Jesus. The enemy works full-time to stop us from realizing who we are in Christ.

> Therefore, [there is] now no condemnation (no adjudging guilty of wrong) for those who are in Christ Jesus, who live [and] walk not after the dictates of the flesh, but after the dictates of the Spirit.
>
> (Romans 8:1 AMP)

This next version should settle the issue of condemnation.

> For those whom He foreknew [of whom He was aware and loved beforehand], He also destined from the beginning [foreordaining them] to be molded into the image of His Son [and share inwardly His likeness], that He might become the firstborn among many brethren. And those whom He thus foreordained, He also called; and those whom He called, He also justified (acquitted, made righteous, putting them into right standing with Himself). And those whom He justified, He also glorified [raising them to a heavenly dignity and condition or state of being]. What then shall we say to [all] this? If God is for us, who [can be] against us? [Who can be our foe, if God is on our side?] He who did not withhold or spare [even] His own Son but gave Him up for us all, will He not also with Him freely and graciously give us all [other] things? Who shall bring any charge against God's elect [when it is] God Who justifies [that is, who puts us in right relation to Himself? Who shall come forward and accuse

or impeach those whom God has chosen? Will God, who acquits us?] Who is there to condemn [us]? Will Christ Jesus (the Messiah), Who died, or rather Who was raised from the dead, who is at the right hand of God actually pleading as He intercedes for us.

(Romans 8:29–34 AMP)

God's word said it, so that settles it! When the enemy brings a charge against you, Jesus is there as your advocate before the Father, saying, "Not guilty." You are not guilty by the blood of Jesus. Did you also notice, in those verses of scripture, that Jesus does not condemn? When the condemnation tries to take root in your heart, just know that the enemy is the one trying to plant it in your mind, not God. God did not send His Son into the world to condemn the world but so that the world, through Him, might be saved. As it is written in John 3:18, "He who believes in Him is not condemned; but he who does not believe is condemned already, because he has not believed in the name of the only begotten Son of God."

Many people believe just the opposite. They think God wants to bring judgment and condemnation. God desires that all men should be saved from destruction. In John 8:2–11 is a story of Jesus dealing with condemnation and showing His love at the same time. There was a woman caught in the act of adultery. Under the law, this would mean the woman would be stoned to death. A group of scribes and Pharisees brought the woman to Jesus. They explained to Jesus that the woman had been caught in adultery. Jesus was reminded that, by the law, the woman should be stoned. They asked Jesus what to do. Jesus told them that the person without sin should be the first to cast a stone. The men departed, convicted in their consciences. Jesus then asked the woman where her accusers were. Jesus asked her if anyone had condemned her. The woman told Jesus that no one had. Jesus told her that he would not condemn her either. Jesus told her to go and sin no more. This story gives no one a license to go out and sin. A person with the right heart will not look for ways to sin but for ways to escape sin. There are two more scriptures I want to cover before I move into how to get rid of the negative thoughts from guilt, shame, and condemnation.

In 1 John 3:20–22, we find strong advice: "For if our heart condemns us, God is greater than our heart, and knows all things. Beloved, if our heart does not condemn us, we have confidence toward God. And whatever we ask we receive from Him, because we keep His commandments and do those things that are pleasing in His sight." So now we know where the condemnation comes from. It comes from the heart. Ultimately the condemnation affects your confidence. Your confidence will then have an effect on your prayers. In 1 Timothy 3:1–6, the requirements for becoming a bishop are considered. Verse 6 hones in on a key point in reference to condemnation. That verse discusses being puffed up with pride and falling into the same condemnation as the devil. Pride will lead you into condemnation. Pride is the opposite of humility. A prideful person is an arrogant person. Pride makes you think you are more important or better than other people. Proverbs 29:23 tells us that pride will bring us low. Proverbs 11:2 tells us when pride comes, then comes shame. Operate in humility, and you will avoid pride. Jesus was a perfect example of humility. Now we will get into how to attack guilt, shame, and condemnation. There are three main ways: repentance, renewing your mind, and speaking the word of God. We will go into detail on each.

Repentance

Before we discuss repentance, we must cover confession. In 1 John 1:9, we read that if we confess our sins, He is faithful and just to forgive us and cleanse us from all unrighteousness. It's not any more complicated than that. Now let's get to repentance.

Repentance is simply making a 180-degree turn away from your sin unto God. Turn away from the sin and turn toward God. Yes, that's the extent of it. Don't make it complicated.

Renew Your Mind

Now let's talk about renewing your mind. "And do not be conformed to this world, but be transformed by the renewing of your mind, that you may prove what is that good and acceptable and perfect will of God," we read in Romans 12:2. The way to renew the mind is through the word of God. That word *transformed* in the previous scripture means *changed*, like the change from caterpillar into butterfly. Now you see what a great change can take place in your life. A heavy dose of the word of God will change the way you think, ultimately changing the way you act. The word of God is food to our spirit.

There is also a scripture, 1 Peter 2:1–2, that refers to the word of God as milk to a new baby: "Therefore, laying aside all malice, all deceit, hypocrisy, envy, and all evil speaking, as newborn babes, desire the pure milk of the word, that you may grow thereby." So get in the word and let it renew your mind and change the way you think. Then you will begin to see spiritual growth. This is not a one-time deal. Feed your spiritual man the word of God like you feed your natural body food. You have to be consistent to see true growth. Consistency is the key to the breakthrough, as my spiritual father used to say.

Speak the Word

Speaking the word of God builds our confidence. Speaking the word of God changes circumstances and situations. Speaking the word of God is a powerful tool for believers. As it is written in Joshua 1:8, "This book of the law shall not depart from your mouth, but you shall meditate in it day and night, that you may observe to do according to all that is written in it. For then you will make your way prosperous, and then you will have good success."

It's very important for us to look at the complete definition of *meditate* before we move on. The original Hebrew meaning of *meditate* is *to murmur, ponder, imagine, speak, study, talk,* or *utter.*

This scripture is telling us that, as a result of murmuring, pondering, imaging, speaking, studying, talking, and uttering the word of God, we will have good success. We have let the enemy destroy the importance of speaking the word. We have heard that it doesn't take all that. We have heard the phrase, "blab it and grab it." What is interesting is that the world has taken these principles from the Bible and used them. No one talks badly about these folks who use these principles. The world has even framed a name for this. The world calls it *positive thinking and speaking.* Can you see the ploy of the enemy to stop us from using these principles that are clearly stated in the Bible?

These next two scriptures will lead us to the end of this book. First, Psalm 45:1: "My heart is overflowing with a good theme; I recite my composition concerning the King; My tongue is the pen of a ready writer." Second, Proverbs 7:1–3: "My son, keep my words, and treasure my commands within you. Keep my commands and live, And my law as the apple of your eye. Bind them on your fingers; Write them on the tablet of your heart."

Two key points emerge here. The tongue is like a pen that is ready to write. The heart is like a tablet. So every time you open your mouth and speak, you are writing on the tablet of your heart. This is important because it is with the heart that we believe. The more we write the word of God on our hearts, the more we believe the word of God. There are several other scriptures in the Bible that mention speaking the word. I think you get the point. So make a decision. You can either speak guilt-ridden, shameful, and condemnation-filled words, or you can speak what God says about the situation. You can choose to speak death or life. I choose life—what about you? You will begin to see a change if you choose the latter. I just thought of one more scripture that will drive my point home.

> If we set bits in the horses' mouths to make them obey us, we can turn their whole bodies about. Likewise, look at the ships: though they are so great and are driven by rough winds, they are steered by a very small rudder wherever the impulse of the helmsman determines. Even so the tongue is a little member, and it can boast of great things. See how much wood or how great a forest a tiny spark can set ablaze! And the tongue is a fire. [The tongue is a] world of wickedness set among our members, contaminating and depraving the whole body and setting on fire the wheel of birth (the cycle of man's nature), being itself ignited by hell (Gehenna). (James 3:3–6 AMP)

Now do you see how powerful the tongue can be? The tongue is so powerful that it can help set the course of your life. Now we can see how these all these work together to defeat the "faith blockers." So we confess our sins, repent, renew our minds, and speak the word of God to get freedom from guilt, shame, and condemnation. Sometimes additional spiritual counseling is required, but these actions will help get you on the road to recovery. Seek any additional counseling through your local faith church. *Faith church* simply means a church that teaches and believes in the whole counsel of God.

Now I want to give you my testimony on the writing of this book before we close with two prayers. I was sitting in a parking lot in the summer of 2005. God began to talk to me in my spirit with a still, small voice. He told me that there are so many of His children who will not step out into what He has called them to do. He said that guilt, shame, and condemnation are the main reasons why people will not step out into their callings. God told me that people are too concerned with the mistakes of the past. He began to show me that all the men and women in the Bible have made mistakes, but He still used them to do great deeds. God named Joseph, Moses, Rahab, Jephthah, David, Gideon, Samson, Paul, Noah, and Abraham. Most of these, other than Jephthah, were names already familiar to me through the Bible.

I began to go back through the Bible and read about these characters again. Sure enough, all of them had flaws. All of them made mistakes at some point in their lives. I wrote all the names down and jotted down notes about each of them as the Lord showed me. I still have the original paper with the names and initial information. My wife was the only one who knew God wanted me to write a book. The thought of writing a book seemed foolish to me. I thought, "I'm not an author. I'm not an English major." I did not immediately step out into this venture. Approximately two years later, I was with a group from my church as we visited another church. A prophet of God, a man I had never seen before, stood before me and said he had a prophetic word for me.

Here is his prophetic word verbatim: "'I've called you to ministry. Every man isn't called to ministry. I've chosen you for these last days, for this last hour, to come into a place with me,' says the Lord. 'Many have overlooked you and thought you were not gifted of God to be able to bring and teach the word. But I chose you even before the foundations of the world. I knew you before you knew you. Therefore I have chosen you. You are going to come forth with a real anointing, a real teaching anointing, and even a real anointing to do the will of God. I decree this day, whatever has been hindering you, delaying you, whatever has been causing you not to come into the flow of your calling, after today, you shall begin to receive a visitation from the Lord.' God shall begin to speak to your heart. He shall begin to open up his kingdom on the inside of you and begin to pour life, rivers of living water, on the inside of you, and everything around you will begin to be affected by your new place in God. And God said, 'I am going to start out with your home, start out with your employment, I'm going to start out with your personal situation. And it's going to put a burning in your soul to pray like never before. You are now getting ready to pray heaven down to your own situation. You don't need to make it known who you are; He will prove who you are. For this day I have ordered your steps. I'm going to bring you before great men,' says the Lord.

"Everything that you have experienced, everything that you have been through that was tough and that was strenuous to your mindset, strenuous to your emotions, strenuous to your heart, God said He has done it to bring forth the birthing of truth." (The next part refers to this book you are reading.) "The Lord said a book is coming. It is not going to be just a book to say you wrote a book. I plan for that book to prosper you, to bring you before great men. I'm planning on that book to have nuggets from heaven that people have never heard before."

I want to thank the late apostle, Johnny B. Watson Jr., of Sure Word Prophetic Ministries, for obeying God and speaking this prophetic word, which has changed my entire walk with God. I can only think how amazing this event was—a definite confirmation that I was supposed to write this book. God knows how to get your attention. It took another seven years before I actually started writing the book. I went through some events in my personal life that were as strenuous to my mindset, my emotions, and my heart as the prophetic word foretold. I actually started writing the book in January 2014. Remember how, at the beginning of the book, I emphasized provision? Well, when I started writing the book, I didn't have the money for publication. God simply told me I didn't have to worry about the money for publishing the book because the book wasn't finished yet. God definitely has a sense of humor. God provided all the money I needed to publish the book by the time it was finished. This was somewhat like Peter stepping out on the water or Abraham stepping out into his God-given call. God is faithful to see you through what He has called you to do. I'm a witness to this fact. Well, my friends, you are now ready to step out into your calling.

Be encouraged as doubt tries to creep into your mind. Read Hebrews 11 if you need a boost to your faith. This chapter tells stories of other men and women doing great deeds for God. I have shown you early in this book how these men and women who were used by God were flawed. Don't let your flaws stop you from being used by God. God is waiting for you to stop making excuses like Moses and just step out and do it. May the Lord God be with you as you start your journey. There is one last matter we must address before you step out. The first step to moving into the purpose God has for your life is to give your life over to Him. Do you feel that purpose tugging on your heart? I want to lead you through a prayer for salvation. Say the following prayer out loud to give your life over to God.

> God, I seek the purpose you have for my life. I know it starts by accepting your Son Jesus Christ as my Lord and Savior. I believe in my heart that Jesus died on the cross for my sins, and was raised again on the third day. I ask you now, Jesus, to save me and come into my heart. In Jesus's name I pray. Amen.

Now here is a prayer to attack guilt, shame, and condemnation.

> Lord, I make a decision right now to rid my thought life of guilt, shame, and condemnation. Your word tells me to forget those things that are behind and reach forward to the high calling of Jesus. I recognize guilt, shame, and condemnation as tools of the enemy to keep me from my calling.

You said in your word that there is no condemnation of those who are in Christ Jesus. I thank you for the shed blood of Jesus Christ that means I am free from condemnation, guilt, and shame. I will continue to renew my mind with your word and change my mindset. I want to thank you, Lord, for setting me free. Whom the Son sets free is free indeed. In the name of Jesus, amen.

About the Author

Ron Momon is a veteran of the United States Air Force and has served in law enforcement for over thirty years. He is an ordained minister and former Associate Pastor of World Restoration Ministries in Decatur, Georgia. Ron enjoys revealing to others the wisdom found in the word of God. He lives in Atlanta, Georgia, with his wife, Renee, and has three adult daughters.

Printed in the United States
By Bookmasters